From Our Kitchens

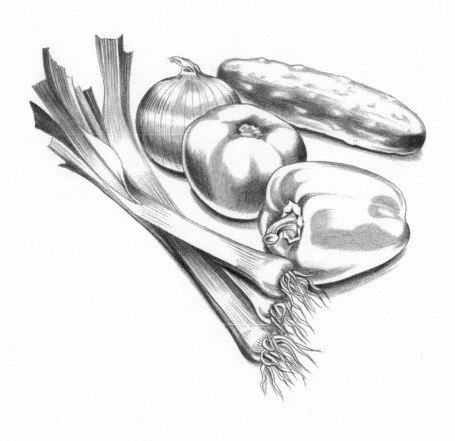

From Our Kitchens

Edited by
Mary Deirdre Donovan

Illustrations by
Mona Mark

VAN NOSTRAND REINHOLD
New York

I(T)P   Van Nostrand Reinhold is an International Thomson Publishing company.
        ITP logo is a trademark under license.

Printed in the United States of America

Van Nostrand Reinhold   International Thomson Publishing GmbH
115 Fifth Avenue   Königswinterer Str. 518
New York, NY 10003   5300 Bonn 3
                                         Germany

International Thomson Publishing   International Thomson Publishing Asia
Berkshire House,168-173   38 Kim Tian Rd., #0105
High Holborn, London WC1V 7AA   Kim Tian Plaza
England   Singapore 0316

Thomas Nelson Australia   International Thomson Publishing Japan
102 Dodds Street   Kyowa Building, 3F
South Melbourne 3205   2-2-1 Hirakawacho
Victoria, Australia   Chiyada-Ku, Tokyo 102
                                         Japan

Nelson Canada
1120 Birchmount Road
Scarborough, Ontario
M1K 5G4, Canada

16 15 14 13 12 11 10 9 8 7 6 5 4 3 2 1

Library of Congress Cataloging in Publication Data

Culinary Institute of America
        From our kitchens / the Culinary Institute of America.
        p.   cm
        Includes index
        ISBN 0-442-01766-9
        1. Cookery. I. Title
        TX714.C832 1993
        641.5—dc20

Table of Contents

Recipes

APPETIZERS AND SALADS

Roasted Garlic and Mustard Vinaigrette
Georgia Peanut Salad Dressing
Tomato-Herb Vinaigrette
Smoked Chicken with Tabbouleh and Tomato-Herb Vinaigrette
Sorrel and Spinach Salad with Avocado and Pistachios
Tagliolini with Smoked Salmon and Fresh Peas
Smoked Duck Salad with Bitter Greens
Seared Scallops with Beet Vinaigrette
Carpaccio of Tuna with Shiitake Salad
Seviche of Scallops
Seviche of Artichoke Hearts
Marinated Roasted Peppers
Gorgonzola Custards
Country-style Duck Terrine
Seafood Sausage with Shrimp and Pistachios

SOUPS

Chicken Broth
Fish Broth
Vegetable Broth
Amish-style Chicken and Corn Soup
Tortilla Soup
Senate Bean Soup
Cuban Black Bean Soup
Borscht
Pan-smoked Tomato Bisque
Pumpkin Soup with Ginger Cream
Chilled Gazpacho

Grilled Flank Steak with Pineapple and Roasted Shallots
Beef Tenderloin with Blue Cheese and Herb Crust
Roast Loin of Pork with a Honey-Mustard Glaze
Pork Tenderloins with Apples and Caraway
Pork with Apricots, Currants, and Pine Nuts
Lamb Chops with Artichokes
Braised Lamb Shanks
Lamb Chops with Sherry-Vinegar Sauce
Calf's Liver, Berlin Style

BEANS AND GRAINS

Bulgur Wheat with Dried Cherries and Apples
Hoppin' John
Curried Braised Lentils with Eggplant and Mushrooms
Three-Bean Stew
Southwest White Bean Stew
Hush Puppies
Timbales of Dirty Rice
Quinoa Pilaf with Red and Yellow Peppers
Lemon Cilantro Rice
Polenta with Parmesan Cheese
Risotto with Asparagus Tips
Wild and Brown Rice Pilaf with Cranberrries
Couscous with Wild Mushrooms and Walnuts
Kahsa with Spicy Maple Pecans
Lentil Ragout
Wild Rice Pancakes

VEGETABLES

Carrot Timbales
Ratatouille
Zucchini Stuffed with Mushrooms and Fennel
Broiled Belgian Endive with Romesco Sauce

Lemon Glaze for Vegetables
Asparagus with Toasted Anchovy, Garlic and Lemon
Steamed Spinach with Garlic and Pernod
Pan-steamed Zucchini and Yellow Squash "Noodles"
Vegetable Tempura
Green Beans with Sun-dried Tomatoes and Mushrooms
Brussels Sprouts with Toasted Walnuts

POTATOES

Candied Yams with Apples and Bananas
Potato Puree with Roasted Eggplant and Garlic
Potato Gratin
Celeriac and Potato Puree
Roësti Potatoes
Potatoes Hashed in Cream
Glazed Sweet Potatoes
Sweet Potato Chips
Sweet Potato Cakes
Oven-roasted Potatoes

DESSERTS

Chocolate Yogurt Mousse
Chocolate Angel Food
Caramel and Pear Polenta Soufflé
Winter Fruit Strudel
Tarte Tatin, St. Andrew's Style
Sweet Ricotta Pastry
Linzertorte
Coffee Granité
Frozen Orange Soufflé
Rum Truffle Torte
Sacher Torte
Petits Pots de Crème
Crème Brulée
Chocolate Sponge Cake
Strawberry Pecan Shortcake
Chocolate Glaze or Sauce
Simple Syrup

Foreword

The title of this book, *From Our Kitchens,* has many meanings for an American cook. On the one hand, it is a straightforward announcement that the recipes are among the most savory and contemporary of all the thousands tested and taught at the kitchens of the Culinary Institute of America, this country's premier cooking school.

On the other hand, this is a compendium of the kinds of recipes Americans really *do* cook in their own kitchens, or would if they had a simple, well-presented recipe. Throughout this splendid volume, the home cook will find everything from southern hush puppies to Tunisian coucous, from roasted chicken cooked as they do in India to Sacher Torte based on the original served in Vienna. For the American kitchen is an open hearth, receptive to many cuisines and techniques, as ready to adapt an ethnic recipe to local ingredients as to repeat a classic right down to the last grain of salt.

Not long ago a leading American cooking magazine defined American cooking as "whatever Americans eat." This, I think, is too facile a statement, not unlike saying that American cars are whatever Americans drive. The truth is that the American kitchen is diverse enough to assimilate traditional regional fare like clam chowder and Key lime pie, immigrant foods like ossobuco and souvlaki, French standards like bouillabaisse and cassoulet, and modern innovations like pizza topped with smoked salmon and sour cream. The best American cooks realize, also, that not everyone can cook everything and that the traditions and culture that make an individual dish a "classic" must be respected and never corrupted.

A French cook knows when he has strayed too far from his French kitchen, and so does a Chinese, Bengali, or Ethiopian chef. American food may incorporate many foreign dishes and seasonings, but serving Tunisian brik, Sephardic boyos and nigirisushi all at one dinner party takes things pretty far afield from American cookery.

From Our Kitchens both acknowledges and respects such distinctions while making accessible some of the world's finest, most exotic dishes to the American table. The recipes for borscht, tandoore morg, polenta, and Linzertorte are exemplary for their clarity, authenticity and taste. If a certain dish takes a good deal of time to prepare, the recipe will say so, but it will never compromise the techniques that make the dish uniquely flavorful. At the same time, these dishes all seem in perfect synch with the way people—at least discerning people—truly enjoy cooking and eating today. There are whole chapters on pasta, pizza and beans—items that in the past would have been slipped into other, broader categories.

These are the kinds of dishes that bespeak the modern kitchen—a kitchen as familiar with the workings of the food processor as with the recommended grams of fat in a healthful diet. I applaud the authors' inclusion of notes on the amount of fat, sodium, calories, cholesterol, protein and fat in each dish, while never sacrificing good taste for some fleeting notion of faddish nutritionism.

This is a truly modern cookbook and a model for all others. The recipes are clear, concise and carefully tested for the home kitchen. The introductory notes at the beginning of each chapter show how concepts of taste and technique have changed in the past decade, freeing the reader from outmoded ideas about what should and should not constitute a good, flavorful soup, gratin or pasta dish. The "preparation notes" are invaluable, and, thank heavens, never chatty. Look at the fine suggestions on how best to preserve and refresh black bean soup or the sensible advice on seasonings given for roasted monkfish with Niçoise olives and Pernod sauce. The "serving suggestions" are just as valuable, giving the reader the traditional way to present a dish as well as a few novel ideas that work just as well.

Yet there is not a whiff of novelty for its own sake in this book. You will not find extravagant, show-off recipes culled from restaurant chefs trying to razzle-dazzle his or her public with unorthodox mixtures and bizarre pairings of ingredients. There is not a single dish in this volume that stretches the bounds of good taste beyond recognition. Dishes like shrimp and herb tortellini with fennel sauce, pork with apricots, currants and pine nuts, kasha with spicy maple pecans, and caramel and pear polenta soufflé are wonderfully evolved from traditional dishes that ethnic cooks would feel immediately comfortable making and consuming. You won't find oddities here like red snapper with strawberries and barbecue sauce or sorbets flavored with chile powder. What you will find are dishes that truly satisfy the palate and do nothing to disturb the digestion. This is what modern cooking is supposed to be about.

What I like best about *From Our Kitchens* is its insistence upon doing things the "right" way as opposed to the "correct" way. So many strides—both technological and culinary—have been made in the preparation of food that the home cook can now accomplish so much more with so much less effort and still turn out superior results. Perhaps this is the book's greatest strength: It is the result of hundreds of thousands of hours of classroom experimentation and refinement based on the firm belief that every aspect of cooking should be looked at, studied, and, when possible, improved upon. As with all the best cookbooks, such as *Joy of Cooking* and *Larousse Gastronomique*, *From Our Kitchens* is not an expression of any one person's individual personality. It is simply—and authoritatively—the expression of aggregate good taste.

John Mariani

Preface

You might think that when professional chefs watch their friends and families work around the kitchen, they are (silently) scoffing at your "amateurish" efforts. Usually, that isn't the case. In fact, most professional chefs have great respect for the talents and skills used in preparing a family meal. After all, no one is a "professional" in a home kitchen.

Home cooks share a common heritage with professionals. Whether in a hotel or at home, on a twelve-burner stove or a two-burner hot plate, with a chef's jacket and toque or a "garden-variety" apron, cooking is the same basic activity. There is no difference in the care and concern that goes into selecting and preparing the best possible fresh ingredient the market has to offer, in the best possible way.

There are some very special problems the home cook must handle daily that could confound even a chef from a 4-star restaurant. Unlike the chef who spends the entire day simmering sauces, chopping herbs, and marinating meats, you are more likely to walk in the door clutching a bag of groceries—to be met by a hungry dog, a ringing phone, and a child who has to leave the house in a hour to make it to a dance class or basketball game. The bunch of arugula you have been dreaming about all the way home provokes an instant cry of "I'm not hungry" from your youngest, who has an aversion to anything green.

The recipes included here, all of which have been adapted from those used in the classrooms of The Culinary Institute of America, have been carefully written with the needs of the home cook in mind. Many of the recipes in this book can be prepared quickly, using such techniques as sautéing, or grilling, or baking. Recipes for updated favorites include pasta dishes that can be easily assembled and pizzas with special toppings. The notes following the recipes should help you adapt them to suit your family's preferences. You can find ingredient substitutions, tips for handling special ingredients, and time-saving suggestions in the Preparation Notes. The Serving Suggestions can recommend dishes to round out a meal or make the dish look as enticing and appetizing as it tastes.

The recipes you choose for a workday dinner will probably be those which you can assemble and cook in under an hour. There are a number of recipes in this collection that may take significantly more time to prepare. Even these dishes offer special time-saving benefits for the cook who can devote an afternoon to working at a more leisurely pace. Although cooking in large batches may take a little longer in the initial assembly and preparation of ingredients, the actual cooking time often remains the same, even when the recipe has been doubled. Whatever you won't need for dinner that night can be frozen, ready to reheat on those nights when your own "TV dinners" are all that stand between you and a commercially prepared version made from rubbery chicken and bland vegetables. While not every recipe can be easily multiplied, several others, such as Cuban Black Bean Soup, Borscht, Beef Goulash, and Enchiladas Verdes, can readily be doubled or tripled.

When you are ready to take the plunge and prepare a festive meal, then you will want to follow some of the guidelines that professional chefs and caterers like to use when preparing special menus.

The most basic key to success is to use the freshest, best quality raw ingredients available. When it comes to fruits and vegetables, anyone who truly loves to cook revels in the brilliant tastes, flavors, and textures of each crop as it comes into the marketplace. The first tender new peas are made all the more delicious when "seasoned" with the realization that they are only at their best for a few short weeks. Unfortunately, we have become so accustomed to having strawberries in February and sweet corn in April that the concept of foods coming in and out of season has been all but lost. There are some clues that will help you identify seasonal foods. They tend to be bountiful, at the peak of flavor and color, and relatively inexpensive. As the price climbs, you will know that the season has nearly come to a close.

Whenever possible, conscientious chefs and home cooks alike will seek out locally grown foods at supermarkets, farmers' markets, and roadside stands. The benefits of this type of shopping have just barely begun to gain recognition. Apart from boosting the local economy, it is also a way to encourage the use of less-invasive farming practices— organically grown foods or those which have been grown with minimal amounts of chemical herbicides, pesticides, and fertilizers. When foods don't have to travel across the country in a refrigerated truck, they can be allowed to ripen on the vine where they can develop the lush flavors and perfect textures that many consumers have forgotten.

Menus don't need to be elaborate to be successful. In fact, simplicity is more often the path to a memorable dining experience than a profusion of courses, side dishes, and sauces. Serve foods that you enjoy cooking and eating, and don't worry about the "right" number of courses.

Know the limitations of time and available work space so that you don't spend the entire day of the event behind the scenes in the kitchen. If you plan a simple first course—say a chilled gazpacho, a tossed salad— then you could perhaps follow up with a main course that is more complex or that requires a little last-minute effort. Then, finish the meal with a simple-to-serve dessert that can be completely prepared in advance, such as a frozen soufflé. Or, concentrate on a more involved first course or a selection of hors d'oeuvre, and choose recipes for the main course and dessert that are as undemanding as possible.

Keep the flavors of the dishes you have chosen in mind. Too many conflicting flavors can confuse the palate. The seasonings of Middle Eastern dishes don't pair up well with Italian flavorings. Try to avoid repeating the same flavor so often that it loses its appeal. Scattering chopped fresh cilantro over everything from the salad to the fish to the rice is bound to deaden the senses. In the same way, a predominance of butter, cheese, in and cream in a soup, in the pasta, and in the dessert will dull the palate.

Each food or dish will have a distinct texture. Just as you should try to create a pleasing array of harmonizing and/or contrasting flavors in the meal, you should try to incorporate a number of different textures as well. Although we tend to concentrate on the way foods look, smell, and taste, the way they feel when we cut or bite into them gives a very special dimension to the meal. Think about how the textures of the accompanying dishes you have chosen will play against the main course you are serving.

A certain harmony is achieved when the meltingly tender meat of an Ossobuco Milanese is paired with a creamy risotto. To avoid overdoing a "soft and creamy" theme, you would then want to search out a bright green vegetable with some snap (green beans, broccoli, or snow peas) as a foil for those textures. A creamy vegetable such as Carrot Timbales might be an excellent counterpoint to the resilient texture and smoky taste of grilled flank steak. A sauce of pineapple and roasted shallots adds yet more textural layers. You may not be conscious of this interplay, but a well-balanced selection of textures is a major factor in creating an overall sense of satisfaction when the meal is finished.

Colors play a role too. With relatively few exceptions, you should aim for a variety of colors. A totally white or brown meal doesn't look as appealing as a plate that combines some of the four basic food color-groups: dark greens; creamy whites or ivory; vivid yellows, oranges, or reds; and rich golds or deep browns. When you follow this guideline, your meals will almost automatically include a good selection of vegetables, grains, or fruits, nicely balancing nutritional and sensory concerns. Foods such as spinach, escarole, carrots, melons, cauliflower, sweet potatoes, beets, and sugar snap peas are visually stimulating. These and other brightly colored fruits and vegetables are also excellent sources of a wide array of nutrients, including vitamins, minerals, proteins, and complex carbohydrates.

USING THE RECIPES

This recipe collection has been selected and prepared with the seasons in mind. The Culinary Institute of America is located in the northeast portion of the country, in the Hudson Valley. We have favored the foods and seasons of our own region: slender asparagus and new peas in May; strawberry shortcake in June; corn and tomatoes in August and September; peaches, apples, and pears beginning in July and on through the fall; pumpkin and squashes for Thanksgiving; root vegetables and dried fruits in the winter months.

Each region of the country will follow its own timetable and have its own special ingredients. Marionberries and succulent salmon are part of the bounty of the Northwest. Crayfish, shrimp, and snapper are the foundation of the gumbos and stews of the Gulf States. Fresh and aged cheeses, orchard fruits, and corn-fed beef laden the tables of the Midwest. Chilies, peppers, and corn have lent Southwestern recipes their special fire and savor. Incorporating the best that your region has to offer into these recipes is one of the best ways to make these recipes reflect your personal cooking style.

Herbs can make simple foods come alive. Fresh chives can be snipped over steaming new potatoes. Shredded mint can be folded into a bowl of chilled melon balls. Slivers of basil can be scattered over sliced sun-ripened tomatoes. Many of our recipes call for herbs, and, unless specifically noted otherwise, we have preferred fresh herbs. What do you do if the fresh thyme in the ingredient list can't be found at your favorite market? First, look for another fresh herb to act as a substitute. Try fresh tarragon to replace dill, or parsley to stand in for cilantro, for instance. When there simply aren't any fresh herbs to be found, dried herbs can be used. The taste is not identical to fresh herbs, but when handled with care, they can do a good job.

Since dried herbs have more concentrated flavors than fresh herbs, remember to add them in small increments earlier in the cooking process than you might add fresh herbs. To expand a dried herb's flavor, some cooks like to sprinkle the herb with a little water and warm it in the microwave for 15 or 20 seconds.

Whether you are working with fresh or dried herbs, remember that the amounts listed in the ingredient list can be modified to suit your taste. But, the only way you will know how much or little you prefer is to taste the food periodically as it cooks and make adjustments as the flavor develops. Adding a little more of an herb or spice is an easy way to put a personal stamp on a recipe. Jot your changes down so that the next time, you'll be able to recreate the flavor or make further modifications.

The following tips and suggestions can help when purchasing foods or working with the recipes to help you get the best results. Unsalted butter is preferred, since it has the freshest, creamiest flavor. If you use salted butter, remember to taste the dish before adding any more salt. When eggs are used, they should be graded large. The broths used in the soups, sauces, and stews were prepared from scratch. If you decide to use canned broths, look for low-sodium brands, and remember to remove any fat from the surface. Dried pastas should be made from durum wheat. Canned beans can be used in place of cooked dried beans; drain and rinse them before adding them to the dish. When using canned fruits, look for brands that are unsweetened or packed in natural juices. Frozen fruits should be frozen whole without any added sugar. Canned and frozen vegetables should be low in sodium or sodium-free.

Some special ingredients called for in these recipes can make a significant difference in the taste of the dish. Extra-virgin olive oil is one such ingredient. Look for the words "extra-virgin" on the label. These oils are a little more expensive, but the added flavor makes them worth the expense. When extra-virgin olive oil is not specified, a good-quality olive or vegetable oil is fine. Balsamic vinegar, another example of these special ingredients, is a wine vinegar that has been allowed to age in wooden barrels. The best brands of balsamic vinegar are produced in the Modena region of Italy. Sun-died or kiln-dried fruits and vegetables have a wonderful rich flavor and are used in recipes in this book for their unique taste. If you can't find them in your area, look for them in mail-order catalogs such as American Spoon Foods or Williams-Sonoma.

Most of the recipes for soups, main dishes, vegetables, and grains will allow the cook a certain degree of latitude in measurements. Adding a little more chopped onion or garlic, an extra handful of carrots, or an extra spoonful of tomato paste is not likely to ruin the end result. If you love spicy chilies or fresh basil, add enough to suit your taste.

There are some ingredients that should be measured with care, especially if you are concerned about holding down the calories, fat, sugar, and sodium in the foods you prepare for yourself and your family. A "splash," "pinch," or "dash" more of items like cheeses, oils, butter, heavy cream, salt, sugar, and syrups can easily affect the nutritional composition of a dish, without making any truly noticeable change in the way the dish tastes.

The nutritional information offered after each recipe is only an approximation. The calculations are based on the number of servings each recipe provides, and the figures were then rounded. These serving sizes may, or may not, meet your family's expectations. In a restaurant, the chef is concerned that each portion be the same size as the next. At home, you may find that "equal" portions aren't reasonable; individual appetites set the standard for serving sizes.

Cooking is both an art *and* a science. Explore, experiment, and enjoy this recipe collection from our kitchens . . . in your own!

Acknowledgments

The educational mission of The Culinary Institute of America is a clear and strong focus for all of us who work together on the Institute team. It has become something of a cliche to say that "we learned a lot about books while we did this last one." still, things don't get to be cliches unless they are true enough to deserve being repeated over and over.

Creating this book, in particular, showed us a whole new side of the book buisiness, and there are many people to thank:

The entire faculty of The Culinary Institute of America, and especially those whose recipes fill the pages of this book;

Pam Chirls, the person who first envisioned this book and who gently but firmly guided it every step of the way;

Mike Suh, whose special efforts resulted in a design that is warmly elegant;

Lorna Smith, the photographer whose talent and perseverance never flagged during what seemed like a ceaseless round of "reshoots";

Our unflappable Marketing Relations Coordinator, Donna Ducker and her counterpart at Van Nostrand Reinhold, Sarah Wolf;

Brad Matthews and the staff in the storeroom;

The editor who gave the raw manuscript its polish, Joy Aquilino, and the editor who obsessed over details like accent marks and the artrist's renderings, Sherrel Farnsworth.

No book is a solo venture, and to all who lent a hand along the way we extend our sincerest thanks.

Appetizers and Salads

1

An appetizer or salad served as a separate first course is a clear signal that the meal will offer more than just food to refuel. It is at least a dining experience, perhaps a special occasion—certainly a celebration of the food itself. We may not always have the time or energy to lavish this kind of attention on a typical lunch or dinner, or on ourselves.

Even a weekday dinner can benefit from the civilizing influence of a separate first course. One of the most appealing and refreshing selections to include in virtually any menu is a salad. This dish clearly illustrates the value of taking the time to carefully select and properly handle food. The actual preparation, though, is simple: Crisp greens, gently rinsed and dried, paired with slivers or slices of fresh seasonal vegetables, toasted nuts, or croutons, can be quickly combined in a single bowl. A homemade vinaigrette is no more difficult to prepare than a salad, and, once mixed, will remain fresh for at least a few days. Bring the salad to the table, toss it with the vinaigrette, and serve it as a separate first course.

You might consider some other easy ways to introduce the main meal. Serve slices of melon with prosciutto, a plate of sliced vine-ripened tomatoes drizzled with olive oil, or an artichoke steamed until tender paired with a vinaigrette for dipping. These dishes are not difficult to prepare and can elevate any meal above the everyday.

A successful first course depends on a number of factors. The appetizer or salad you select should have some relationship with or connection to the dishes that will follow. It is also important to keep in mind that this is the first course—not the "main event." Keep the serving size small enough to take the edge off an appetite.

As the prelude to all that will follow, the appetizer should be made from the freshest and most delicious raw ingredients you can find. This does not mean the most expensive, by any means. While a big can of beluga caviar is always welcome, simple seasoned foods can be just as satisfying. A dish of fresh peas, just minutes out of your own garden or fresh from a local greenmarket or farmer's produce stand, quickly steamed and served with nothing more than a knob of sweet butter, a sprinkle of salt, and a dash of freshly ground black pepper, is assuredly one of the more exquisite starts to any meal.

The recipes in this chapter are primarily intended for those special gatherings of friends and family, when you can make the time to carefully plan a menu and its sequence of courses. A variety of foods are featured, from shellfish to red peppers. Wherever possible, substitutions are noted for ingredients that might not be available, either because of geographic location or season, or because the cost is prohibitive.

THE TOOLS

Every kitchen should be equipped with the tools that make cooking easier and more pleasant. The most basic tool is the knife. A small selection of knives, including a chef's knife, a paring knife, and a bread knife, will enable you to prepare virtually any recipe in this chapter. Filleting or boning knives, which are used to cut up fish or poultry, are also good to have on hand. Because knife brands vary in quality, each manufacturer's line has a slightly different balance or feel. Before you purchase your knives, be sure to take the time to hold each one in your hand, making certain they feel comfortable. Also, look for knives with "full tangs." This means that the blade of the knife extends through the entire length of the handle. The knife will feel more substantial in your hand and will last longer.

If you plan to prepare the duck terrine or the seafood sausage, a meat grinder is a good idea. A food processor can also be used. The terrine should be prepared in a 2-pound mold. Earthenware molds are traditionally used, but an enameled cast-iron version is an excellent alternative. If you don't have a special terrine mold, you can substitute any loaf pan; the one you use to prepare meatloaf would be fine.

Any attention you lavish on your greens will be rewarded when you sit down to a crisp, refreshing salad. Thorough rinsing (to remove all sand and grit) and careful drying are two crucial preparation steps. One special piece of equipment that you might want to consider purchasing, if you don't already have one, is a good-quality salad spinner. Look for a centrifugal spinner with a smooth action that is sturdy enough to stand up to regular use. If you enjoy cooking with fresh herbs, a smaller version for rinsing and drying herbs is also a good investment.

An instant-reading thermometer is another wise investment. These thermometers are inserted into foods as they cook, and the temperature registers very quickly on a small dial or digital readout. Look for them in gourmet or cookware shops, the housewares sections of department stores, or restaurant supply houses.

Roasted Garlic and Mustard Vinaigrette

This dressing is a good choice for salads made with assertive greens (romaine, arugula, or radicchio, for example) or as a marinade for grilled vegetables. The garlic can be roasted anytime that the oven is already on. An exact temperature or cooking time is not important, as long as the garlic develops a rich, brown color and the flesh becomes soft enough to mash easily.

Makes about 1 cup, or enough for 10 individual salads

4 cloves of garlic, roasted and peeled
4 teaspoons Dijon-style mustard
½ teaspoon salt
¼ teaspoon freshly ground or cracked black pepper
1 teaspoon honey
¾ cup vegetable oil
¼ cup cider vinegar

IN ADVANCE   Roast an entire garlic bulb in a 350 to 375°F oven for about 40 minutes, or until the juices have turned a rich brown color and the cloves are very soft with a rich, sweet aroma.

1.   Place the garlic in a small mixing bowl and mash it with the back of a fork.

2.   Add the mustard, salt, pepper, and honey to the garlic and blend well with a whisk to form a smooth paste. Add the oil in a stream, whisking constantly.

3.   Add the vinegar to the oil mixture, whisking constantly until it is thoroughly blended. The vinaigrette can be used immediately, or can be stored in the refrigerator for up to 5 days.

PREPARATION NOTES

The unused garlic can be reserved easily. Peel the remaining cloves and place them in a jar. Cover them with a good-quality cooking or salad oil and store in the refrigerator until needed.

If the vinaigrette has been refrigerated, allow it to return to room temperature before serving it, and whisk it vigorously to properly recombine all of the ingredients.

SERVING SUGGESTIONS

• Any roasted garlic not used in this vinaigrette can be added to a number of other dishes. For a delicious hors d'oeuvre, or as an alternative to a traditional garlic bread, drizzle pizza dough (your own or prepared) with a puree of olive oil and the roasted garlic, and bake in a hot oven until the dough is cooked.

• For a simple and satisfying pasta dish, sauté a few cloves in extra-virgin olive oil, then toss with drained cooked pasta, plenty of cracked black pepper, chopped fresh herbs, and grated Parmesan cheese.

Nutritional information, per serving (1½ tablespoons): 150 calories; trace of protein; 16 grams fat; 2 grams carbohydrate; 145 milligrams sodium; 0 milligrams cholesterol.

Georgia Peanut Salad Dressing

A "natural" peanut butter—prepared without any added sugar—is the best choice for this vinaigrette. Choose a good-quality peanut oil, one with a clean, pleasant, and intense "peanut" aroma.

Makes about 1 cup, or enough for 10 individual salads

1 tablespoon peanut butter
1 tablespoon tightly packed brown sugar
1 tablespoon chopped fresh herbs (parsley, tarragon, and/or chives)
½ teaspoon finely minced garlic
½ teaspoon salt
¼ teaspoon freshly ground black pepper
5 tablespoons malt vinegar
¾ cup peanut oil

1. Blend the peanut butter, brown sugar, herbs, garlic, salt, and pepper to a smooth paste in a small mixing bowl.

2. Whisk the vinegar into the peanut butter mixture until evenly blended.

3. The vinaigrette can be used immediately, or may be stored in the refrigerator for up to 5 days.

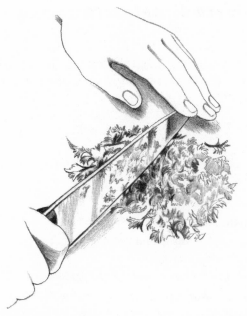

If the vinaigrette has been refrigerated, allow it to return to room temperature before serving it, and whisk it vigorously to properly recombine all of the ingredients.

SERVING SUGGESTIONS

• After tossing the salad with this dressing, sprinkle it with chopped dry-roasted or plain peanuts.

• Try this vinaigrette drizzled over stir-fried vegetables or cooked grains or pasta. It also makes an excellent dipping sauce for crudité.

Nutritional information, per serving: 160 calories; trace of protein; 17 grams fat; 2 grams carbohydrate; 115 milligrams sodium; 0 milligrams cholesterol.

Tomato-Herb Vinaigrette

This exceptionally low-calorie, low-fat dressing has a rich flavor and a substantial texture. If your diet can accommodate a few extra calories or grams of fat, add a little extra-virgin olive oil along with the herbs to finish the vinaigrette.

Makes about 1 cup, or enough for 10 individual salads

2 teaspoons olive oil
2 teaspoons shallots, minced
1 garlic clove, minced
2 tablespoons tomato paste
2 cups tomatoes, peeled, seeded, and chopped (fresh or canned)
freshly ground black pepper to taste
2 tablespoons fresh herbs (one or more of the following: basil, dill,
*   tarragon, chives, cilantro, thyme, flat leaf parsley), chopped*
1 tablespoon balsamic vinegar (or more to taste)

1. Heat the olive oil in a skillet over medium heat. Add the shallots and garlic. Sauté, stirring frequently, until they are tender and translucent, about 3 to 4 minutes.

2. Add the tomato paste and sauté for another 3 to 4 minutes, stirring constantly.

3. Add the chopped tomatoes and continue to cook over medium heat for about 10 minutes, or until the mixture is thickened and reduced.

4. Remove the tomato mixture from the heat, let cool slightly, and puree it in a blender until very smooth. Add the pepper, herbs, and vinegar and puree until evenly blended.

5. If the vinaigrette is too thick, add a little water (or use broth or tomato juice if available). The vinaigrette should pour easily from a spoon. Taste the vinaigrette and add more vinegar to taste if necessary.

6. Refrigerate the vinaigrette until you are ready to use it.

PREPARATION NOTES

The vinaigrette can be prepared through step 4 (omitting the addition of the fresh herbs) and then frozen for up to 2 to 3 months. So, if you have a large quantity of tomatoes to use, you can double or even triple the batch. When ready to serve, add fresh herbs and taste the vinaigrette to see if it requires additional seasoning.

SERVING SUGGESTION

This vinaigrette, which is featured in the recipe for Smoked Chicken with Tabbouleh (page 10), also makes an excellent dressing when paired with leftover cooked pasta and assorted vegetables for a quick pasta salad.

Nutritional information, per serving (about 1½ tablespoons): 20 calories; trace of protein; 1 gram fat; 3 grams carbohydrate; 10 milligrams sodium; 0 milligrams cholesterol.

Smoked Chicken with Tabbouleh and Tomato-Herb Vinaigrette

Tabbouleh is a grain salad, popular in Middle Eastern cuisines. It is prepared from bulgur wheat, a cracked wheat that is usually easy to find along with rice and other grains in larger supermarkets. Or, look for it in health food stores or food cooperatives.

Makes 4 servings

⅓ cup bulgur wheat
½ cup tepid water
¼ cup finely diced scallions
¼ cup minced flat-leaf parsley
2 tablespoons minced mint leaves
2 teaspoons extra-virgin olive oil
1 tablespoon lemon juice, freshly squeezed
½ teaspoon grated lemon zest
3 drops Tabasco sauce
6 ounces smoked chicken breast, thinly sliced
1 plum tomato, quartered
½ cup Tomato-Herb Vinaigrette (see page 8)

IN ADVANCE   Prepare the Tomato-Herb Vinaigrette.

1.   Soak the bulgur wheat in the water for about 40 minutes. Drain the bulgur of any excess water and set aside.

2.   Combine the scallions, parsley, mint, olive oil, lemon juice and zest, and Tabasco sauce. Whisk well to combine. Pour the dressing over the bulgur and stir to mix evenly. Refrigerate the tabbouleh for several hours or overnight.

3.   When ready to serve, mound the tabbouleh on a chilled platter or individual plates. Arrange the sliced chicken breast and quartered tomato around the tabbouleh. Drizzle with Tomato-Herb Vinaigrette.

If fresh mint is unavailable, use an additional tablespoon of parsley. You can also substitute smoked turkey for the chicken breast if desired.

The tabbouleh can be prepared in larger quantities and served with grilled or sautéed poultry or seafood.

SERVING SUGGESTIONS

In addition to the tomatoes, you can accompany the salad with other vegetables, either raw (cucumbers, jicama, bell peppers, tomatoes, and carrots) or chilled steamed or blanched (broccoli, cauliflower, green beans, and peas). As accompaniments, pass a bowl of tamari dipping sauce or hummus and a basket of toasted or grilled pita bread.

Nutritional information, per serving: 180 calories; 16 grams protein; 6 grams fat; 17 grams carbohydrate; 45 milligrams sodium; 40 milligrams cholesterol.

Sorrel and Spinach Salad with Avocado and Pistachios

Sorrel is a tart green with a lemony taste. The peak seasons for sorrel are spring and summer. These sharply flavored greens were once revered for their curative powers, especially as part of a spring "elixir." Today, sorrel is often available year-round from greenhouses.

Makes 4 servings

8 ounces fresh spinach leaves, well-rinsed
4 ounces fresh sorrel leaves, well-rinsed
1 ripe avocado
2 garlic cloves, finely minced
minced zest and juice of 1 lemon
2 tablespoons walnut oil
¼ teaspoon salt (or to taste)
freshly ground pepper to taste
¼ cup shelled pistachios

1. Tear the spinach and sorrel leaves into bite-sized pieces and place in a salad bowl.

2. Remove the peel and pit from the avocado and slice it into a separate bowl. Add the garlic, lemon zest and juice, and walnut oil; toss well. Season with salt and pepper.

3. Add the avocado mixture to the greens and toss lightly until the leaves are lightly coated with the oil.

4. Sprinkle the salad with the pistachios and serve on chilled plates.

For this recipe, use a ripe Haas avocado. It should have slightly glossy, dark, pebbly skin. To determine whether it is ripe, cradle the avocado in the palm of your hand and squeeze very gently; it should yield only slightly. If the avocados in your market are a little too firm, you can speed up the ripening process by keeping them in a closed paper bag (at room temperature) for just a day or two.

SERVING SUGGESTIONS

This salad would make an excellent introduction to any main course that features salmon or catfish. See Catfish Topped with Crabmeat and Cornbread Crumbs (page 96) as an example.

Nutritional information, per serving: 205 calories; 4 grams protein; 19 grams fat; 10 grams carbohydrate; 185 milligrams sodium; 0 milligrams cholesterol.

Tagliolini with Smoked Salmon and Fresh Peas

You might occasionally be able to purchase smoked salmon scraps for slightly less than sliced smoked salmon. Since for this recipe you will be cutting the salmon into slivers anyway, perfect slices are not necessary. Make sure, however, that the salmon is of good quality: It should have a smooth, mellow flavor, neither oily nor harsh.

Makes 6 servings

½ recipe Basic Pasta Dough (see page 66)
2 tablespoons unsalted butter
1 tablespoon finely minced shallots
1 garlic clove, finely minced
⅓ cup dry white wine
1 teaspoon minced pepperoncini
½ cup heavy cream
2 ounces smoked salmon, cut into strips
½ cup green peas (fresh or frozen)

IN ADVANCE Have a pot of water ready to cook the pasta and bring it to a boil as you start to prepare the sauce.

1. Roll the pasta into thin sheets and cut into *tagliolini* (thin noodles). Set aside.

2. Heat the butter in a skillet over medium heat. Add the shallots and garlic; sauté them until the shallots are translucent, about 3 to 4 minutes.

3. Raise the heat to high and add the wine to the skillet. Reduce the liquid to about two-thirds of its original volume (about 3 minutes).

4. Add the pepperoncini and heavy cream and reduce the heat to low. Continue to simmer while cooking the pasta.

5. Drop the tagliolini into a pot of boiling salted water and cook until *al dente,* about 2 to 3 minutes. Drain the pasta well, and place into a heated bowl.

6. Add the salmon and peas to the skillet and simmer just until the peas are a very bright green. Pour the sauce over the pasta and toss to coat. Serve at once.

PREPARATION NOTES

The sauce may be prepared up to 24 hours in advance through step 4 and stored in the refrigerator until needed. The pasta may also be rolled, cut, and cooked in advance. After the pasta is drained, rinse it well with very cold water, and then toss it gently with a little olive oil to prevent the strands from sticking. When ready to serve, heat the sauce and add the salmon and peas. Heat the pasta separately in about 1 inch of boiling water.

If you prefer, prepared pasta (either dried, or a refrigerated fresh pasta) may be used in place of homemade pasta.

SERVING SUGGESTIONS

• This dish would also make an excellent dinner entrée. The recipe would serve about three to four people when accompanied with a crisp salad and some crusty bread.

• Pass with plenty of freshly grated Parmesan cheese and freshly ground black pepper.

Nutritional information, per (appetizer) serving: 235 calories; 6 grams protein; 12 grams fat; 22 grams carbohydrate; 200 milligrams sodium; 45 milligrams cholesterol.

Smoked Duck Salad with Bitter Greens

This recipe includes instructions for preparing a small smoke-roaster to cook the duck. However, you can reduce the amount of work (and smoke in your house) by purchasing a good-quality smoked duck breast.

Makes 8 servings

¾ pound boneless skinless duck breast
6 cups greens (frisée, arugula, romaine, and/or radicchio)
½ cup Georgia Peanut Salad Dressing (see page 6)
¾ cup diced bell peppers (green, yellow, and/or red)
½ cup corn kernels
½ cup diced cucumber
½ cup peeled, seeded, and diced plum tomato
1 tortilla, cut into strips, toasted

IN ADVANCE   Preheat the oven to 350°F.

To prepare a smokebath, use a small skillet with an ovenproof handle and proceed as follows: Scatter hardwood chips (mesquite, apple, or hickory) in the bottom of the skillet and place a rack over the chips. If the skillet does not have a tight-fitting lid, use aluminum foil.

1.   Place the duck breast on the rack in the skillet. Cover the pan tightly with a lid or foil. Place the pan over high heat just until the aroma of smoke is apparent; then, place it into the preheated oven and roast for about 3 minutes.

2.   Remove the duck to a baking dish and cook for another 10 to 12 minutes, or until the meat is cooked through but still slightly pink.

3.   Place the lettuce in a large bowl. Pour the dressing over the greens and toss until all of the leaves are well-coated. Lift the greens from the bowl with a slotted spoon, allowing the excess dressing to drain back into the bowl. Place the drained greens in a salad bowl or mound on individual plates.

4.   Slice the duck into julienne or dice and add it to the excess dressing in the first bowl, along with the peppers, corn, cucumber, and tomato. Toss until all of the ingredients are evenly coated with the dressing.

5.   Place the duck mixture on top of the greens, and sprinkle with the toasted tortilla strips.

PREPARATION NOTES

To toast the tortilla, heat an unoiled skillet over medium high heat. Add the tortilla to the pan and allow it to cook until lightly toasted on both sides. Remove it from the pan and cut it into strips while the tortilla is still warm. Reserve them until they are needed.

SERVING SUGGESTIONS

Replace the Georgia Peanut Salad Dressing with the Roasted Garlic and Mustard Vinaigrette to complement the rich flavors of this dish.

Nutritional information, per serving: 100 calories; 8 grams protein; 4 grams fat; 7 grams carbohydrate; 50 milligrams sodium; 25 milligrams cholesterol.

Seared Scallops with Beet Vinaigrette

Since you will need to sear the scallops just before they are served, prepare an entrée that doesn't require a great deal of last-minute attention, such as the Roast Loin of Pork with Honey-Mustard Glaze (see page 142).

Makes 4 servings

2 medium beets
2 tablespoons cider vinegar
4 teaspoons extra-virgin olive oil
¼ cup stock or broth (chicken or vegetable)
1 tablespoon chopped fresh dill leaves
¼ teaspoon salt
⅛ teaspoon freshly ground black pepper
½ pound sea scallops
½ cup grated carrots
½ cup grated daikon radish
½ bunch watercress or arugula

1. Prepare the beet vinaigrette as follows: Trim the beets, leaving about 2 inches of stem still attached to each beet. Cook the unpeeled beets in simmering water for about 30 minutes, or until they can be easily pierced with the tip of a paring knife. Remove the beets from the water and allow them to cool until they are easy to handle.

2. Slip the skins from the beets, or cut them away with a paring knife. Grate the beets directly into a mixing bowl. Add the vinegar, olive oil, stock, dill, salt, and pepper and mix. In a food processor or blender or with immersion blender, puree the vinaigrette until very smooth. Chill until needed.

3. Remove the muscle tabs from the scallops and pat them very dry with absorbent toweling. Heat a non-stick skillet or well-seasoned cast iron pan over medium-high heat. Add the scallops and sear for about 1 minute on each side. For the best results, the scallops should not touch one another during cooking, so if necessary, work in batches to avoid overcrowding the pan.

4.   Pool about 3 tablespoons of the vinaigrette on each serving plate, then add the scallops, grated carrots and daikon, and a few sprigs of watercress or arugula.

PREPARATION NOTES

To streamline the preparation of this appetizer, prepare the beet vinaigrette the day before. If daikon is unavailable, grated red radishes may be substituted. Enoki (or straw) mushrooms would also look attractive with this dish. Simply trim the stems and arrange them on the plate.

SERVING SUGGESTIONS.

• By increasing the amount of scallops to ¾ pound, this appetizer could easily become a light entrée.

• Prepare a selection of vegetables, including steamed new peas or green beans, grilled zucchini, yellow squash, and/or eggplant, or a portion of Potato Gratin (page 226) to round out the meal.

Nutritional information, per 2-ounce serving: 110 calories; 10 grams protein; 5 grams fat; 6 grams carbohydrate; 300 milligrams sodium; 25 milligrams cholesterol.

Carpaccio of Tuna with Shiitake Salad

In its original version, *carpaccio* was prepared with thinly sliced, raw lean beef and served with a piquant sauce. In this adaptation, the beef is replaced with raw tuna, which has a rich red color similar to beef. The tuna must be perfectly fresh, and it is a good idea to ask if the fish is "sushi grade." Sushi grade means that the fish is exceptionally fresh. In a process similar to preparing seviche, the acids in the sake will chemically "cook" the fish before it is served.

Some of the ingredients mentioned here may be difficult to find in a supermarket. Look for a market that carries Asian groceries as a source for wasabi ("green horseradish" powder), tamari sauce, and vegetables such as bok choy and enoki mushrooms.

Makes 4 servings

1/4 cup rice wine vinegar
2 tablespoons soy or tamari sauce
3 ounces shiitake mushrooms, stems removed, thinly sliced
1/2 cup thinly sliced carrots, briefly steamed
1/4 cup red onion, julienned
1/2 cup finely shredded bok choy
6 ounces fresh tuna fillet, sliced very thin
1 tablespoon sake
2 tablespoons plain yogurt (low-fat or nonfat)
1 teaspoon wasabi powder

IN ADVANCE Steam or boil the carrots until tender-crisp, then drain and cool thoroughly.

1. Place the rice wine vinegar and 1 tablespoon of soy sauce in a bowl. Add the shiitakes, carrots, onion, and bok choy, and toss to coat all ingredients evenly. Refrigerate for about 30 minutes.

2. While the shiitake salad is marinating, place the tuna slices in a shallow dish and brush them with sake. Marinate in the refrigerator for several minutes.

3. In a separate bowl, combine the yogurt and wasabi powder with the remaining soy sauce.

4. Arrange the tuna slices on a chilled platter or individual plates. Drizzle the wasabi sauce over the tuna and mound some of the shiitake salad in the center of each slice.

PREPARATION NOTES

A very sharp knife is crucial in order properly slice the tuna. Chilling the tuna thoroughly before slicing will also make it easier to cut even, neat slices. Or ask the fish vendor to slice the tuna for you.

SERVING SUGGESTIONS

Be sure to chill the plates for this dish before serving. If you have time, place the tuna slices on chilled plates, then cover them with plastic wrap and spread them very thinly over the entire plate by pressing and flattening the tuna with your fingertips. The red of the tuna makes an elegant background for the shiitake salad.

Nutritional information, per serving: 110 calories; 13 grams protein; 2 grams fat; 10 grams carbohydrate; 275 milligrams sodium; 25 milligrams cholesterol.

Seviche of Scallops

You can use other fish to prepare this dish, including tuna, swordfish, squid, or monkfish. The important point is to select fish that is perfectly fresh. One with a relatively firm texture, similar to scallops, would be the best choice.

Makes 4 servings

½ pound sea scallops
2 tablespoons lime juice, freshly squeezed
1 tablespoon extra-virgin olive oil
1 teaspoon minced jalapeño (fresh or canned)
1 garlic clove, minced fine
¼ teaspoon salt
⅛ teaspoon freshly ground black pepper
2 plum tomatoes
½ small red onion
1 scallion
4 teaspoons chopped fresh cilantro or parsley

1.   Remove the muscle tabs from the scallops and slice them into thin rounds.

2.   Combine the lime juice, olive oil, jalapeño, garlic, salt, and pepper in a bowl and whisk to blend well. Add the sliced scallops and toss to coat evenly. Cover the bowl and place it in the refrigerator overnight or for about 8 hours before serving.

3.   As close as possible to the time you wish to serve the seviche, prepare the vegetables for garnish: Peel and seed the tomato and cut it into neat dice or julienne (see Preparation Notes below); cut the onion into very thin slices and separate into rings; cut the scallion very thinly on the bias.

4.   Fold the cilantro or parsley into the seviche. To serve, mound it on a chilled platter or individual plates and scatter the tomato, onion, and scallion on top.

To peel a tomato, first cut out the stem end using a paring knife, and cut an "X" in the blossom end. Drop the tomato into rapidly boiling water. Remove it after 30 to 45 seconds and drop it into a bowl of ice water. Once it is cool enough to handle the skin should peel away easily. Plum tomatoes are then cut in half from stem end to blossom end, and the seeds scooped out and discarded. Beefsteak or slicing tomatoes are cut in half across the belly and the seeds are squeezed out.

SERVING SUGGESTIONS

• Serve avocado slices or guacamole as an accompaniment to this dish, and garnish the plates or platter with additional sliced tomatoes and sprigs of cilantro.

• To prepare guacamole, simply mash the flesh of a ripe avocado and add a few drops of lime juice and a little salt and freshly ground pepper to taste.

Nutritional information, per serving: 90 calories; 10 grams protein; 4 grams fat; 5 grams carbohydrate; 295 milligrams sodium; 25 milligrams cholesterol.

Seviche of Artichoke Hearts

When you select artichokes in the market, look for firm globes that are uniformly sized. They should have firm, plump stems that are not withered or puckered, and the leaves should form a tight head.

Makes 4 servings

4 artichokes
2 lemon slices
1 plum tomato, peeled, seeded, and diced
1 tablespoon lime juice, freshly squeezed
4 teaspoons extra-virgin olive oil
½ cup julienned red onion
½ teaspoon jalapeño, finely chopped (or to taste)
1 scallion, split and sliced thinly on the bias
1 garlic clove, finely minced
1 tablespoon chopped fresh cilantro

1. Trim the stems, leaves, and fuzzy "choke" from the artichokes. Place the hearts in a small pot with enough water to cover generously. Add the lemon slices and simmer until the artichoke hearts are very tender, about 12 to 15 minutes. Cool the hearts and slice thinly or quarter.

2. Combine the artichokes with the remaining ingredients. Toss until evenly blended and allow the seviche to marinate for at least 2 hours or overnight in the refrigerator.

3. Taste the seviche just before serving and adjust the seasonings with additional cilantro, lime juice, coarsely ground black pepper, and salt to taste.

4. Serve the seviche chilled or at room temperature.

Artichokes hearts that have been frozen or packed in brine can be used instead of fresh artichokes.

SERVING SUGGESTIONS

• To make a quick guacamole to serve with the seviche, mash the flesh of a ripe avocado with chopped tomato, minced jalapeño, and sliced scallions. Add a spoonful of lime or lemon juice, and salt and pepper to taste.

• For a more "festive" plate, place dollops of guacamole on slices of tomato, or scoop out halved cherry tomatoes and fill them with the guacamole.

Nutritional information, per serving: 55 calories; 1 gram protein; 3 grams fat; 6 grams carbohydrate; 33 milligrams sodium; 0 milligrams cholesterol.

Marinated Roasted Peppers

If you stumble across a great deal on bell peppers, this recipe can easily be doubled, or even tripled. The Serving Suggestions on the following page offer a number of ways to present this dish.

Makes 8 servings

4 sweet bell peppers (red, yellow, orange, purple, and/or green)
½ cup extra-virgin olive oil
¼ cup balsamic vinegar
2 tablespoons chopped fresh basil
1 teaspoon minced garlic
¼ teaspoon salt
⅛ teaspoon ground black pepper

1. Halve the peppers and place them cut-side down on a lightly oiled baking sheet. Broil the peppers until they are evenly blackened. Remove them from the broiler and immediately cover the baking sheet with an inverted baking pan. Allow the peppers to "steam" for 10 to 15 minutes, or until they are cool enough to handle easily.

2. To make the marinade, combine the remaining ingredients in a bowl and whisk to blend well.

3. Peel the skin from the peppers. If necessary, use a paring knife as to remove any skin that does not peel away easily. Remove and discard the seeds and ribs. Cut the peppers into strips and add them to the marinade.

4. Marinate the peppers overnight in the refrigerator before serving.

PREPARATION NOTES

A colorful mix of peppers will make a more appealing presentation. When red and yellow peppers are difficult to find or too expensive, use green peppers and add a few strips of jarred or canned pimentos.

• Mound the peppers on a chilled appetizer plate. Make Parmesan curls by shaving a block of the cheese with a swivel-bladed vegetable peeler.

• Top the marinated peppers with a scattering of toasted pine nuts, dried currants that have been plumped in warm water, and crumbled fresh goat cheese or grated aged goat cheese.

• This colorful relish can be served as an accompaniment to a terrine or sausages, or as a topping for pizza.

Nutritional information, per serving: 130 calories; trace of protein; 14 grams fat; 3 grams carbohydrate; 70 milligrams sodium; 0 milligrams cholesterol.

Gorgonzola Custards

Gorgonzola is an Italian blue cheese. When ripe, it has a creamy texture. As it ages, it becomes drier and more crumbly. Other blue cheeses can be used in place of the Gorgonzola, including Roquefort, Saga Blue, or Maytag Blue.

Makes 6 servings

2 tablespoons unsalted butter
½ cup diced onion
1½ cups half-and-half
3 whole eggs
3 ounces Gorgonzola or other blue-veined cheese, crumbled
freshly ground pepper to taste

IN ADVANCE Preheat the oven to 275°F. Boil water for the water bath. Very lightly oil six 3-ounce custard cups.

1. Heat the butter in a skillet over medium heat. Add the onions and sauté them until they are limp and translucent, about 5 minutes. Stir them frequently as they sauté, and do not allow them to take on any color. Remove them from the skillet to a mixing bowl and allow them to cool.

2. Add the half-and-half, eggs, cheese, and pepper to the onions, and whisk to combine.

3. Ladle the custard mixture into lightly oiled custard cups. Place them in a deep baking dish or casserole and add enough hot water to come up to the level of the custard.

4. Cook the custards in a 275°F oven until a blade inserted in the center of a custard comes out clean, about 25 to 30 minutes.

5. Serve the custards directly in the molds, or unmold them onto warmed plates if desired.

These custards can be mixed and poured into prepared molds on the morning of a dinner party. Since they can be served hot or warm, consider baking the custards an hour or so ahead of time so they can cook gently at the proper temperature without complicating the preparation of the other items on the menu that might require a hotter oven temperature. Maintaining a slow, gentle cooking temperature is crucial to the finished custards' silky, delicate texture.

SERVING SUGGESTIONS

• As a first course, this rich dish should be followed by a simple grilled entrée accompanied with plenty of bright fresh vegetables.

• Serve this dish after the entrée, as a cheese course to end the meal, with a glass of good port, toasted walnuts, and ripe pears.

• To create an interesting contrast of textures, unmold the custards onto large croutons made as follows: Cut out rounds of bread the same size as the opening of the custard cup, and toast them lightly under a broiler. If desired they might be brushed with a little clarified butter first.

Nutritional information, per serving: 210 calories; 8 grams protein; 18 grams fat; 4 grams carbohydrate; 260 milligrams sodium; 180 milligrams cholesterol.

Country-style Duck Terrine

Country-style terrines have a coarse texture and a robust flavor. Terrines are traditionally served directly in the earthenware baking dish. In fact, the dish's name is the same as that of the baking dish itself.

Makes one 2-pound terrine

1 duckling (with the liver reserved)
2 to 3 teaspoons salt
¼ teaspoon ground black pepper
4 tablespoons brandy
1 to 2 tablespoons unsalted butter
½ cup finely chopped onion
1 clove garlic, finely minced
3 tablespoons chopped fresh herbs (parsley, chives, tarragon, chervil, and/or basil)
6 ounces fatback, cubed
1 whole egg
⅓ cup coarsely chopped pistachio nuts

IN ADVANCE Place the bowl and steel blade for the food processor and a mixing bowl into the freezer to chill. Assemble the meat grinder and prepare a terrine mold (refer to the Preparation Notes for detailed instructions).

1. Remove the breast meat from the duck. Dice half of the breast. (Use the remaining duck breast in another recipe.) Place the diced meat in a bowl and sprinkle it with 1 teaspoon of the salt and all of the ground pepper. Add 2 tablespoons of the brandy and toss to coat. Refrigerate until needed.

2. Heat the butter in a skillet over medium heat and sauté the onion and garlic, stirring frequently, until they are limp and translucent. Transfer this mixture to a bowl, then stir in the herbs and fatback. Freeze this mixture for about 20 minutes, or until the fatback starts to firm.

3. Remove the leg meat from the bones and dice it finely. Add this meat to the fatback mixture along with the duck liver and remaining brandy and salt. Stir until the ingredients are evenly combined. Grind this mixture through a meat grinder with a medium die.

4. Place about one-third of the ground mixture in the bowl of a food processor along with the egg. Puree until the mixture is smooth (it should remain cold). Transfer this to a chilled bowl.

5. Gently fold in the diced breast meat and pistachio nuts and immediately place in a prepared terrine mold. Place the mold in a deep roasting pan and set it on the center rack of the oven. Add about 3 inches of boiling water to make a hot water bath.

6. In a 250°F oven, bake the terrine to an internal temperature of 140°F, for about 1 hour. The temperature of the water bath should remain at approximately 170°F. Adjust the oven temperature as necessary throughout cooking time.

7. Remove the terrine from the water bath and allow it to cool to room temperature before refrigerating.

8. Slice the terrine thinly and serve with a variety of garnishes and sauces (see below for suggestions).

PREPARATION NOTES

To prepare the terrine mold, line it with sheets of thinly sliced fatback or plastic wrap. Allow enough "overhang" on all sides so that the excess can be folded back over the top of the filled terrine. Once it is filled, remove any air pockets by "chopping" a knife or spatula vertically through the terrine with an up-and-down motion for its entire length. Then drop the filled mold onto the work surface from a height of about 4 to 5 inches.

Sauté or grill the duck breast that is not used in this recipe, slice it thinly on the bias, and add it to a salad as a garnish or include it in an impromptu pasta dish.

SERVING SUGGESTIONS

Country-style terrines are typically served with a variety of condiments, including special mustards, thin slices of dark rye or pumpernickel breads, cornichons, and pickled onions.

Nutritional information, per slice: 165 calories; 5 grams protein; 15 grams fat; 3 grams carbohydrate; 535 milligrams sodium; 100 milligrams cholesterol.

Seafood Sausage with Shrimp and Pistachios

While the sausage in this recipe is formed with plastic wrap, it can also be prepared with lamb casings. These can occasionally be obtained from your butcher or the meat department of large grocery stores. If you do find casings, be sure to rinse them thoroughly to remove all salt by slipping one end over the faucet and allowing the water to run through.

Makes 2 pounds of sausage (about 20 links)

2 slices of white bread, crust removed, diced
3 egg whites, lightly beaten
1 cup heavy cream, well-chilled
¾ pound flounder fillet, diced, chilled
½ teaspoon salt
¼ teaspoon paprika
¼ teaspoon ground coriander seed
⅛ teaspoon cayenne pepper
¼ pound shrimp, peeled, deveined, and diced
1 cup shelled pistachio nuts
2 teaspoons chopped fresh parsley, chives, chervil, or dill

IN ADVANCE   Place the bowl and steel blade for the food processor and a mixing bowl into the freezer to chill.

1.   Combine the diced bread, beaten egg whites, and ¼ cup of the heavy cream. Stir until the bread is evenly moistened. Refrigerate this mixture until needed.

2.   Place the diced fish in a food processor. Add about 2 tablespoons of crushed ice. Process the fish and ice until a coarse puree forms. The mixture should still feel very cold.

3. Add the chilled bread-and-cream mixture and the spices to the fish puree, and continue to puree just until all the ingredients are evenly blended and the mixture appears smooth.

4. With the food processor still running, add the remaining heavy cream gradually by pouring it through the feed tube. Remove this mixture to a chilled bowl.

5. Fold in the shrimp, pistachios, and chopped herbs gently, just until all the ingredients are evenly dispersed throughout the mixture.

6. Place a sheet of plastic wrap on a work surface. Mound the sausage along the long end of the wrap, then roll it up in jelly-roll fashion. Take care not roll the plastic into the sausage mixture. Twist the end to seal the sausage in place, and tie it with twine to hold the shape.

7. Poach the sausage in barely simmering water (170°F) to an internal temperature of 150°F (about 12 to 15 minutes). Remove the sausage roll from the water and immediately place it in ice water. Once cool, remove the sausage and wrap it in fresh plastic wrap. Store it in the refrigerator until ready to serve.

8. Remove the wrapping and slice the sausage neatly. Serve with a sauce or condiments.

PREPARATION NOTES

The key to success is making certain that all ingredients and tools are kept well-chilled during preparation.

This recipe can also be prepared with up to a half pound of one or more of the following items: Bay or sea scallops, muscle tabs removed; Crabmeat, picked to remove all bits of shell; Lobster meat, quickly blanched, then diced.

SERVING SUGGESTIONS

• A freshly prepared mayonnaise flavored with saffron, roasted garlic, or pureed red peppers would make a good accompaniment.

• Slice the sausage thickly, grill it just long enough to mark each slice, and serve with a tomato coulis flavored with tarragon and horseradish.

• Sauté the sausage slices in a little heated butter, and serve them on bed of sautéed leeks and fennel.

• Wrap the entire sausage in puff pastry, brioche dough, or phyllo dough and bake until the pastry is golden brown.

Nutritional information, per serving: 140 calories; 10 grams protein; 10 grams fat; 4 grams carbohydrate; 219 milligrams sodium; 66 milligrams cholesterol.

Soups

2

We look to soup for nourishment, comfort, and ease of preparation. When we decide to serve a soup, either as a part of the meal or as the main course, there are a few things to consider. First, what season of the year is it? For example, a brimming bowl of Pan-smoked Tomato Bisque is wonderful in the late summer when tomatoes are at their peak. A hearty Senate Bean Soup is perfect for winter's dark nights. And a light, zesty Chilled Gazpacho cools us off on the most blistering summer day.

Soups have been traditionally thought of as a way to wring the last bit of nourishment and flavor from other foods, and they do satisfy that requirement admirably. However, they should not be the final stop for food that is past its prime. Remember that your soup will only be as good as what you put into it.

Most soup recipes are extraordinarily forgiving and can be easily adapted to meet the needs of the moment, particularly when you need to improvise ingredients. For example, a broth-based soup with lots of fresh vegetables can usually accommodate a few beans or lentils, for a more hearty main-course soup. You can double, or even triple, most recipes to prepare batches to eat now and freeze for later. You can even decide to serve a soup chilled instead of hot.

While simmering most soups for 10 or 15 minutes longer than the recommended cooking time won't normally make a big difference, it is

important to know that soups can be overcooked, leaving them flat and tasteless. Pureed soups, or those that include ingredients like beans and potatoes, can scorch easily. Check your soup, as it simmers, by tasting it from time to time. Stop cooking it just as soon as you like the way it tastes and all of the ingredients are properly tender.

The recipes in this chapter reflect a variety of soup styles. Some are thick and creamy, others are rich broths garnished with plenty of fresh vegetables and herbs.

Among a soup's most important elements is the liquid it is "built" upon. A wonderful broth is at the heart of many of these soups, and you will find recipes in this chapter to prepare three basic broths. If they are prepared in large batches and frozen for later use, they can become a staple "convenience" frozen food that eliminates the need for prepared canned broth or bouillon cubes, as well as the fat or sodium they might contain. Both vegetable and fish broths can be prepared from start to finish in just under an hour.

Rich, homemade broths may be served with whatever you have on hand in the refrigerator for a quick lunch or Sunday evening supper: a little chopped meat; some leftover cooked grains, vegetables, or beans; a splash of tomato juice; a sprinkling of fresh herbs and a big crouton.

Chicken Broth

If you can find a stewing hen, substitute it for the bones called for in the ingredient list. You will be rewarded with a broth that has an intense aroma and tangible body.

Makes about 2 quarts

4 pounds chicken bones
3 quarts cold water (or as needed)
1 large onion, sliced thin
1 carrot, sliced thin
1 celery stalk, sliced thin
5 to 6 whole black peppercorns
3 to 4 parsley stems
1 bay leaf
1 sprig fresh thyme

1. Place the chicken bones in a large pot. Add the cold water. (The bones should be under at least 2 inches of water.) Bring the water slowly to a boil over medium heat.

2. As the water comes to a boil, skim any foam that rises to the surface. Once a boil is reached, lower the heat to establish a slow, lazy simmer.

3. When the broth has simmered for about 1½ to 2 hours, add all of the remaining ingredients. Continue to simmer for another hour, skimming the surface as necessary.

4. Ladle the broth through a sieve into a clean container. Allow the broth to cool to room temperature and then store under refrigeration for up to 5 days, or freeze it for up to 3 months.

This broth can also be made with the carcasses of roasted birds (you will need about three for this recipe.) Remove all of the meat from the bones. Then, either make the broth immediately, or store the bones in freezer containers in the freezer for up to 2 months. If you want to make broth and don't have any bones stored in the freezer, you can often find necks, backs, and wings in the meat department of your supermarket to use in this recipe.

SERVING SUGGESTIONS

If you chill the broth overnight in the refrigerator, any fat that wasn't skimmed away will have risen to the surface and hardened, making it easy to remove. The broth will then be completely fat-free, and will contain only the salt that you choose to add yourself.

Nutritional information, per cup: 20 calories; 2 grams protein; trace of fat; 1 gram carbohydrate; 10 milligrams sodium; 1 milligram cholesterol.

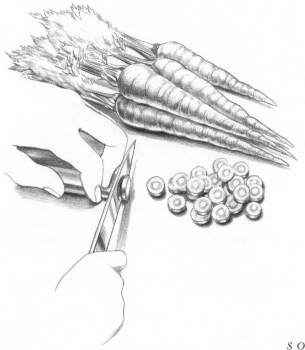

Fish Broth

This broth is a healthful "convenience" food that can help make meal preparation a snap at the end of a long day. Its recipe—as well as that for the vegetable and chicken broths—multiplies easily if you have a good quantity of ingredients on hand. Once the correct cooking temperature has been reached, a gallon of stock takes no longer to simmer than a quart. Then you will be able to store what you don't need right away in the freezer.

Makes about 1 quart

1 tablespoon vegetable oil
2½ pounds fish bones and/or crustacean shells
1 onion, sliced thin
1 leek, trimmed and sliced thin
1 celery stalk, trimmed and sliced thin
½ cup mushrooms or mushrooms stems, sliced thin (optional)
½ cup dry white wine (optional)
5 cups cold water
1 sprig fresh thyme, tarragon, or dill
2 to 3 parsley stems
1 bay leaf
3 to 4 black peppercorns

1. Heat the oil in a saucepan. Add the fish bones and/or shells, onion, leek, celery, and mushrooms. Stir until all the ingredients are evenly coated with oil. Cover the pot and cook without stirring over low heat for about 5 minutes.

2. Add the wine (if using), and simmer until the wine is reduced by half. Then add the water and the remaining ingredients. Bring the broth to just below a simmer, and continue to cook over low heat for 35 to 45 minutes.

3. Strain the broth through a sieve. Discard the bones, vegetables, and herbs.

The fish bones or shells—from shrimp, crab, or lobsters—used to make this stock should be perfectly fresh. If you don't have enough ingredients or time to make a batch right away, you can freeze the bones or shells for up to 6 weeks in freezer containers.

If you do not need the broth right away, cool it completely before refrigerating it. The refrigerated shelf-life of this broth is about three days. If frozen, label and date the containers and be sure to use the stock within 4 to 6 weeks. Bring the broth to a full boil before using it. This will make it easy to spot any spoilage before you have added it as an ingredient in another dish.

SERVING SUGGESTIONS

Fish broth can be used to prepare risotto or pilafs of various grains, which can then be garnished with, or served as an accompaniment to, a variety of seafood dishes.

This broth can also be used as the basis for a fish stew, such as Cioppino (see page 98).

Nutritional information, per cup: 20 calories; 4 grams protein; 1 gram fat; 1 gram carbohydrate; 10 milligrams sodium; trace of cholesterol.

Vegetable Broth

The vegetables listed below as ingredients should be thought of merely as suggestions. Feel free to add or substitute other vegetables, as long as they will not give the finished broth a strong odor or color (for example, beets and their greens might not be appropriate). Starchy vegetables may make the broth foam over as it simmers. Beyond that, let your taste be your guide.

Makes about 2 quarts

2 teaspoons olive or corn oil
1 to 2 garlic cloves, finely minced
2 teaspoons minced shallots
2 quarts water
½ cup dry white wine or vermouth (optional)
1 large onion, sliced thin
1 leek, trimmed and sliced
1 celery stalk, sliced thin on the bias
1 carrot, sliced thin
1 parsnip, sliced thin
1 cup broccoli stems, sliced thin
1 cup sliced fennel (with some tops)
4 to 5 whole black peppercorns
½ teaspoon juniper berries
1 bay leaf
1 sprig fresh thyme (or ¼ teaspoon dried)

1. Heat the oil in a large saucepot over medium heat. Add the garlic and shallots, and sauté, stirring frequently, until they are translucent, about 3 to 4 minutes.

2. Add the remaining ingredients, and over medium heat slowly bring the broth to just under a boil. Reduce the heat to low.

3. Simmer the broth for about 30 to 40 minutes, or until it has developed a good, rich flavor.

4. Strain the broth through a sieve, then allow it to cool completely before storing it in the refrigerator.

PREPARATION NOTES

This broth can be prepared in large batches and frozen for later use. Be sure to label and date the containers so that you are sure to use the oldest broth first.

When preparing vegetables for other dishes, save any wholesome trim or peels that you want to put into the broth. Save them up in a container, then every few days, start a new pot of broth. Your recipes will get a nutritious boost, and you'll avoid the use of canned broths that might be higher in sodium than you'd like.

SERVING SUGGESTIONS

In place of water or chicken broth, use this broth to prepare grain or bean dishes, in soups and stews, or as the cooking liquid for pan-steamed vegetables.

Nutritional information, per cup: 14 calories; 1 gram protein; trace of fat; 2 grams carbohydrate; 10 milligrams sodium; 0 milligrams cholesterol.

Amish-style Chicken and Corn Soup

Amish cooking has always been noted for its use of herbs and spices. The saffron in this soup lends it a deep golden color as well as a subtle flavor. If you prefer, the soup can be prepared without the saffron. The difference in taste is minimal.

Makes 8 servings

½ stewing hen or fowl, cut into pieces
2 quarts chicken stock or broth
¾ cup onion, coarsely chopped
½ cup carrots, coarsely chopped
½ cup celery, coarsely chopped
1 teaspoon crushed saffron threads
¾ cup corn kernels (fresh or frozen)
½ cup celery, finely diced
1 tablespoon chopped fresh parsley
1 cup cooked egg noodles

1. Combine the stewing hen with the stock, onions, carrots, celery, and saffron. Heat the stock to a simmer and cook for about 1 hour, skimming the surface as necessary.

2. Remove the stewing hen from the broth and set aside until it is cool enough to handle. Pick the meat from the bones and dice it.

3. Strain the broth through a fine sieve.

4. Add the reserved diced chicken, corn, celery, parsley, and cooked noodles to the broth. Reheat the soup to a simmer and serve immediately.

This soup can be completed through step 3 in advance: The broth and diced chicken meat can be refrigerated for 2 to 3 days, or frozen for up to 3 months. Store them in separate containers and label and date them. To serve, heat the broth to a full boil, then add the diced meat and remaining ingredients to complete the soup.

Stewing hens (or fowls) are the best choice for soups. They are more mature and fully flavored than fryers or broilers, and the result is a soup that has a wonderfully rich flavor and body. You can use an entire bird to prepare a gallon of broth, then freeze the broth and cooked meat you won't need for this recipe in separate containers for later use in other soups or recipes.

SERVING SUGGESTIONS

• This soup could easily be served as a Sunday dinner. Accompany it with a hearty bread, such as a whole grain or sourdough, or make big popovers.

• Instead of making a salad to round out the meal, you might want to prepare pita bread stuffed with sliced avocado, fresh tomato, and red onion. Tuck a few sprouts into the pocket for some "crunch."

Nutritional information, per serving: 110 calories; 13 grams protein; 2 grams fat; 10 grams carbohydrate; 65 milligrams sodium; 25 milligrams cholesterol.

Tortilla Soup

This soup can be served as the center of a light meal, and rounded out with a green salad. Toasting the corn tortillas before grinding them will fully enhance their flavor.

Makes 6 servings

4 corn tortillas
6 cups chicken broth
1 garlic clove, finely minced
¾ cup finely grated or pureed onion
¾ cup tomato puree
1 tablespoon fresh cilantro leaves, chopped
1 teaspoon ground cumin
1½ teaspoons mild chili powder
1 bay leaf
½ cup shredded cooked chicken breast, boneless, skinless
2 tablespoons grated cheddar cheese
½ cup diced avocado

IN ADVANCE   Preheat the oven to 300°F.

1.   Cut the tortillas into matchstick-sized strips. Place them in an even layer on a baking sheet and toast them in 300°F oven for about 15 minutes. Or, toast the strips by sautéing them in a dry skillet over medium heat, tossing frequently. Reserve about ½ cup of the strips for garnish. Crush the remainder in a food processor or blender.

2.   Heat about 2 tablespoons of the broth in a soup pot. Add the garlic and onion and sauté over medium-high heat stirring frequently, for about 5 to 6 minutes, or until they release a sweet aroma.

3.   Add the tomato puree and continue to sauté the mixture for another 3 minutes. Add the cilantro, cumin, and chili powder and sauté for another 2 minutes.

4. Add the remaining chicken broth, crushed tortillas, and bay leaf. Stir well and bring the soup to a simmer. Continue to simmer over low to medium heat for about 25 to 30 minutes. Strain the soup through a sieve or put through a food mill.

5. Serve the soup in heated bowls and garnish with the shredded chicken, cheddar cheese, diced avocado, and reserved tortilla strips.

PREPARATION NOTES

The shredded chicken should be gently warmed in a small amount of the hot soup, either in a small saucepan over medium heat, or in the microwave for 40 seconds at 80% power.

Avocado will turn brown if it is cut very far in advance. Avoid cutting the avocado more than 1 hour before you will need it, then sprinkle the diced flesh with a little lemon or lime juice and toss to coat. Cover the avocado and keep it refrigerated until needed.

This soup can be prepared in advance through step 4. Once strained and cooled, it may be refrigerated for about 2 to 3 days, or frozen for about 2 months. To reheat the soup, bring it to a full boil and thin if necessary with a little stock.

SERVING SUGGESTIONS

• If avocados are not in season or unavailable, substitute peeled, seeded, and diced tomatoes or cucumbers.

• Instead of making tortilla strips for a garnish, cut the tortilla into wedges and toast them in the oven. Mash the avocado with a little lime juice and some diced tomato to make guacamole. When ready to serve, place a dollop of the guacamole on each of the tortilla wedges and float these "croutons" on top of the soup. Scatter grated cheddar cheese over all. Omit the shredded chicken if desired.

Nutritional information, per serving: 150 calories; 12 grams protein; 5 grams fat; 16 grams carbohydrate; 50 milligrams sodium; 15 milligrams cholesterol.

Senate Bean Soup

According to legend, this soup was frequently served in the dining room of the United States Senate. One summer, it was taken off the menu when the hot weather arrived. There was such a hue and cry, however, that it soon reappeared. To make certain that they would never again be deprived of their favorite soup, the Senate actually passed a bill requiring that it be served every day the dining hall was open.

Makes 8 servings

1¼ cup dried navy beans
½ onion, cut into small dice
¾ cup carrots, cut into small dice
2 celery stalks, cut into small dice
1 garlic clove, finely minced
4 cups chicken or vegetable broth
1 smoked ham hock
1 tablespoon vegetable oil
1 white potato, cut into large dice
3 to 4 whole black peppercorns
1 whole clove
½ teaspoon salt (or, to taste)
½ teaspoon ground black pepper (or, to taste)
Tabasco sauce, to taste

IN ADVANCE Rinse and sort the beans to remove any stones or moldy beans. Then use *one* of the following methods to prepare them for the recipe:

• Soak the beans overnight in enough cool water to cover generously.

• Place the beans and enough water to cover in a pot. Bring to a boil, then remove from the heat and allow to soak for 1 hour. Drain the beans before continuing.

1. Heat the oil in a large saucepan over moderate heat. Add the onions, carrots, celery, and garlic and sauté over low to medium heat for about 5 minutes, or until the garlic has a sweet aroma and the onions are a light golden brown.

2. Add the prepared beans, broth, and ham hock to the pan. Add enough water to cover the beans by about 1 inch. Simmer for about 30 minutes.

3. Add the potato, peppercorns, and clove. Continue to simmer the soup over low heat for another 30 minutes, or until the beans and potatoes are tender enough to mash easily.

4. Remove the ham hock from the soup. When it is cool enough to handle easily, pull the lean meat away from the bone and dice it. Reserve this meat to add to the soup as a garnish.

5. Puree about half of the soup in a food processor or blender until smooth, then return it to the pot. Add salt, pepper, and Tabasco sauce to taste.

6. Serve the soup very hot, in heated bowls or cups. Scatter a little of the reserved diced ham over each serving.

PREPARATION NOTES

This soup can be prepared in advance through step 5, and refrigerated for up to 3 days or frozen for up to 2 months. The diced meat for garnish may be held separately, or added to the soup before it is stored. When reheating, be sure to return the soup to a full boil. As bean soup tends to thicken while stored, you may need to thin this soup with a little broth or water. It may also be necessary to adjust the seasonings.

SERVING SUGGESTIONS

A traditional accompaniment to this soup is garlic-flavored croutons.

Nutritional information, per serving: 160 calories; 11 grams protein; 2 grams fat; 25 grams carbohydrate; 370 milligrams sodium; 0 milligrams cholesterol.

Cuban Black Bean Soup

Allspice, so named because it blends the flavors of several different spices—cinnamon, clove, and nutmeg—is actually the pea-sized berry of an evergreen pimento tree native to the West Indies and South America. Its whole berries give this soup its special flavor.

Makes 8 servings

1½ *cups dried black beans, soaked overnight*
5 *cups chicken or vegetable broth*
1 *whole clove*
2 to 3 *allspice berries*
⅛ *teaspoon cumin seeds, toasted*
¼ *teaspoon dried oregano leaves*
4 to 5 *whole black peppercorns*
¼ *teaspoon salt*
1 *yellow onion, diced*
1 *green pepper, diced*
1 *garlic clove, finely minced*
1 *tablespoon dry sherry*
1 *tablespoon lemon juice, freshly squeezed*
1 *cup finely shredded fresh spinach leaves*

IN ADVANCE Rinse and sort the dried beans to remove any stones or moldy beans. Use *one* of the following methods to prepare them for the recipe:

• Soak the beans overnight in enough cool water to cover generously.

• Place the beans in a pot and add enough water to cover. Bring to a boil, then remove from the heat and allow to soak for 1 hour. Drain the beans before continuing.

If desired, the clove, allspice, cumin, oregano, and black peppercorns may be tied into a small cheesecloth bundle, called a "sachet."

1. Combine the beans, broth, clove, allspice, cumin, oregano, salt, and peppercorns. Simmer for about 40 minutes, or until the beans are nearly tender.

2. Heat 2–3 tablespoons of broth or water in a pot. Add the onion, green pepper, and garlic. Stew them over low heat, stirring from time to time, for about 6 to 8 minutes, or until tender.

3. Add the stewed vegetables to the beans and continue to simmer until the beans are tender enough to mash easily, an additional 10 to 12 minutes. If you tied the spices in a sachet, remove at this time.

4. Puree about one-third of the beans in a food processor or blender, then return it to the pot.

5. Add the sherry, lemon juice, and shredded spinach, and simmer for an additional minute before serving.

PREPARATION NOTES

This soup may be prepared through step 4, then cooled and refrigerated for up to three days or frozen for up to 2 months. In this case, before completing step 5, reheat the soup to a full boil. If the soup is too thick, add enough stock or water to reach the desired consistency (thick, but still liquid enough to pour easily from a ladle).

SERVING SUGGESTIONS

Black bean soup is typically garnished with cooked rice that has been tossed with a little vinaigrette, some chopped scallions, and minced garlic. If desired, serve a wedge of lemon or lime on the side.

Nutritional information, per serving: 160 calories; 12 grams protein; 1 gram fat; 26 grams carbohydrate; 80 milligrams sodium; trace of cholesterol.

Borscht

Many Eastern European countries lay claim to a special beet soup. One traditional recipe calls for the shredded beets to ferment for several days, giving the soup its sour flavor. Here, a splash of red wine vinegar is used. Borscht can be served hot or cold, as a first course, or as a one-course supper. Check the serving suggestions following the recipe for ideas.

Makes 4 servings

5 whole beets
4 cups chicken, beef, or vegetable broth
1 clove garlic, finely minced
½ cup julienned or diced onions
½ cup julienned or diced leeks
½ cup finely shredded white cabbage
⅓ cup julienned or diced celery
2 dill sprigs
2 to 3 parsley sprigs
3 to 4 whole black peppercorns
¼ teaspoon whole fennel seeds
2 tablespoons red wine vinegar (or to taste)
½ teaspoon salt (or to taste)
¼ teaspoon ground black pepper (or to taste)
¼ cup sour cream

IN ADVANCE Remove the leaves from the dill and parsley sprigs. They can be finely chopped, then sprinkled over the soup before it is served.

1. Peel and dice the beets, place them in a pot with half of the stock, and simmer over low heat for about 15 minutes, or until the beets are tender.

2. Remove the beets from the heat and reserve their cooking broth.

3. Combine the garlic, onion, and leeks with about ¼ cup of the remaining broth. Cover the pot and cook gently over low heat until the onions are limp. Add the cabbage, celery, dill and parsley sprigs, peppercorns, and fennel seeds. Simmer over low heat for 20 minutes, or until the cabbage is tender.

4. Add the beets and their cooking broth to the soup, and simmer for an additional 5 to 6 minutes.

5. Just before serving the soup, add the vinegar and salt and pepper to taste.

6. Serve the soup very hot with a dollop of sour cream and a sprinkling of chopped dill and parsley leaves.

PREPARATION NOTES

This soup may be prepared in advance through step 4. Once the soup has cooled, it can be refrigerated for up to 3 days or frozen for up to 2 months. Be sure to return the soup to a full boil before serving it after extended storage.

SERVING SUGGESTIONS

• Borscht can be served cold or hot. If desired, garnish a julienne or dice of cooked beef brisket and/or duck breast meat.

• This soup may also be pureed to a smooth consistency (after having been completed through step 4).

Nutritional information, per serving: 70 calories; 5 grams protein; 1 gram fat; 10 grams carbohydrate; 195 milligrams sodium; trace of cholesterol.

Pan-smoked Tomato Bisque

We tend to think of bisques as being made exclusively from shellfish such as lobster or shrimp. It wasn't always that way, however. The name, "bisque," reflects the fact that this style of soup, no matter what the basic ingredients, was thickened with a dry biscuit. Today, the interpretation of terminology is less strict. This bisque shares little with the first bisques, except for a rich, slightly textured consistency.

Makes 6 servings

2 cups chicken or vegetable broth
1 yellow onion, cut into small dice
1 celery stalk, cut into small dice
1 leek, white and light green portions, cut into small dice
2 cups chopped plum tomatoes (fresh or canned)
1 cup tomato puree
2 ounces sun-dried tomatoes, chopped
1 tablespoon chopped fresh thyme leaves
¼ cup long-grain white rice, uncooked
3 tablespoons balsamic vinegar
1 plum tomato, peeled, seeded, diced, and pan-smoked

IN ADVANCE   To pan-smoke the tomatoes, scatter a few wood chips in the bottom of a skillet. Place a rack over the chips, and set a plate on the rack. Put the diced tomatoes on the plate, and cover the skillet tightly. (Use aluminum foil if a tight-fitting lid is not available.) Place the pan over high heat until you can smell smoke. Remove the pan from the heat and keep covered for an additional 3 to 4 minutes.

1.   Heat about ¼ cup of the broth in a soup pot over medium-high heat. Add the onion, celery, and leek. Cover the pot and cook for about 4 to 5 minutes. The vegetables should start to release their own juices.

2.   Add the remaining broth, plum tomatoes, tomato puree, sun-dried tomatoes, and thyme leaves. Simmer for 30 minutes.

3. Add the rice and continue to simmer for another 15 minutes. Remove the soup from the heat, let cool slightly, and puree it in a blender or with an immersion blender until very smooth.

4. Return the soup to the pot. Stir in the pan-smoked tomatoes and reheat to just below a boil. Serve at once in heated soup bowls.

PREPARATION NOTES

To give the bisque an extremely fine texture, strain it through a sieve after pureeing.

To make a Roasted Tomato Bisque, slice 2 tomatoes in ¼-inch slices, lay them on an oiled sheet pan, and roast them in a 400°F oven for about 20 minutes. Substitute the sun-dried tomatoes with the roasted tomatoes, and omit the pan-smoked tomatoes in the last step.

SERVING SUGGESTIONS

This soup may be served with large croutons. Thinly slice good-quality French or Italian bread, and trim or shape the slices so that they will fit easily into the soup bowls. Then toast the slices on a baking sheet in a hot oven for about 10 minutes, or until golden brown.

Nutritional information, per serving: 115 calories; 5 grams protein; 3 grams fat; 22 grams carbohydrate; 60 milligrams sodium; trace of cholesterol.

Pumpkin Soup with Ginger Cream

Look for plain pumpkin pieces in the frozen-food section of your supermarket. Canned pumpkin will not work quite as well in this recipe, although it can be used if fresh or frozen pumpkin is unavailable.

Makes 6 servings

2 teaspoons butter
1 yellow onion, cut into small dice
1 celery stalk, cut into small dice
2 teaspoons fresh ginger root, minced
2 to 3 garlic cloves, minced
3 cups diced pumpkin (fresh or frozen)
1 cup sweet potatoes, peeled and sliced
5 cups vegetable or chicken broth (or water)
1 small cinnamon stick
1/4 teaspoon freshly ground nutmeg (or to taste)
1/2 teaspoon salt
2 teaspoons lime juice, freshly squeezed
1/2 cup dry white wine
1/2 cup evaporated skim milk
1/2 cup chilled heavy cream, whipped

1. Heat the butter in a soup pot over medium heat. Add the onion, celery, half of the ginger root, and the garlic. Sauté the mixture, stirring occasionally, for about 8 to 10 minutes, or until the onion and celery are limp.

2. Add the pumpkin, sweet potatoes, broth, cinnamon stick, and nutmeg. Simmer until the pumpkin is very tender, for about 30 minutes.

3. Remove the soup from the heat and let cool slightly. Puree the soup in a blender or food processor or with an immersion blender until quite smooth.

4.   Return the soup to medium heat. Add the salt, lime juice, wine, and evaporated milk. Stir to combine well and reheat the soup to just below a boil.

5.   Whip the heavy cream to medium peaks and fold in the remaining ginger root.

6.   Serve the soup in heated soup bowls and garnish each portion with a dollop of ginger-flavored cream.

PREPARATION NOTES

For an exceptionally fine and smooth texture, the soup may also be strained through a fine sieve after pureeing.

SERVING SUGGESTIONS

• This soup could also be garnished with a scattering of toasted pumpkin seeds.

• For an elegant presentation, add a tablespoon of diced, cooked lobster meat to each serving.

Nutritional information, per serving: 145 calories; 8 grams protein; 6 grams fat; 28 grams carbohydrate; 300 milligrams sodium; 20 milligrams cholesterol.

Chilled Gazpacho

This soup can be made as smooth, or left as chunky, as you prefer. The recipe can be easily doubled or tripled, but keep in mind that this soup stays at its best for only about 24 hours, and does not freeze well.

Makes 4 servings

4 or 5 plum tomatoes, coarsely chopped
1 medium-sized cucumber, peeled, seeded, and diced
1 small yellow onion, minced
1 cup fennel, diced
½ cup red pepper, diced
½ cup rich chicken broth or stock
4 teaspoons balsamic vinegar
1 tablespoon tomato paste
1 tablespoon extra-virgin olive oil
1 clove garlic, finely minced
1 tablespoon fresh tarragon leaves, chopped
¼ teaspoon Tabasco sauce

1. Combine all of the ingredients in a food processor or blender, and puree until the mixture has reached a relatively uniform but coarse consistency.

2. Chill the soup overnight to allow the flavors to mature.

3. Serve the soup in chilled bowls or cups.

If desired, some of the feathery tops of the fennel can be reserved for a garnish. Be sure that they have been well-rinsed and dried, then chop them finely.

SERVING SUGGESTIONS

There are several ways to garnish gazpacho. Try setting out several bowls filled with fresh chopped vegetables, including red and green peppers, scallions, cucumber, celery, and fennel, and croutons. Then everyone can dress up their gazpacho to suit his or her taste.

Nutritional information, per serving: 100 calories; 4 grams protein; 4 grams fat; 15 grams carbohydrate; 20 milligrams sodium; trace of cholesterol.

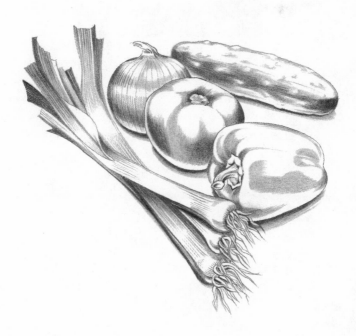

Pasta and Pizza

3

It is hardly news that Italian cuisine has become an integral part of everyday eating in the United States. Pasta and pizza—simple, "peasant" foods that offer the busy cook an excellent way to make quick, easy meals—are among the most popular. The sauces or toppings you choose can be as elaborate or as simple as you like—the meal is a guaranteed success.

Both pasta and pizza are based on doughs that are simple to prepare from inexpensive ingredients that are easy to have around the house. If you prefer, though, you can purchase pizza crusts in a variety of forms: fresh dough that you shape yourself, partially baked frozen crusts, or packaged pizza crusts that are sold along with other bread items in most grocery stores.

Fresh pasta can be found in the refrigerated or frozen-food cases of most supermarkets. Dried pastas of excellent quality and in a variety of shapes, sizes, colors, and flavors are also widely available. Having pasta and pizza on hand in the pantry or freezer means that you can prepare a delicious, satisfying appetizer or hors d'oeuvre, light meal, or snack in less time than it takes to have a pizza delivered to your door.

The basic recipes for both pizza and pasta dough call for flours that may be a little more difficult to find than ordinary all-purpose flour.

The best flours for making fresh pasta are semolina, durum, or manitoba flours. These are considered "hard" wheat varieties, and are responsible for the slightly resilient texture we associate with good-quality pasta. These flours can often be found in gourmet food shops, Italian delicatessens, through mail-order houses, and in larger super-markets. However, if you cannot find them, bread flour is a satisfactory substitute. Bread flour has slightly more protein than all-purpose flour, so if you cannot find bread flour, compare labels and purchase the brand with the most grams of protein per cup.

There are some "pantry staples" that are good to have on hand so that you can improvise your own pizza or pasta sauces or toppings. Olive oil, sun-dried or canned whole or crushed tomatoes, cured olives, capers, dried wild mushrooms, anchovies, and artichoke hearts are just a few. With a generous reserve of garlic and onions and a chunk of fresh Parmesan cheese, you will be able to whip up something satisfying at virtually a moment's notice. If you like, you can then embellish this simple fare with ingredients like *prosciutto, pancetta,* bacon, *chorizo* or other cured sausage, heavy cream, butter, and any enticing fresh herbs and vegetables you might see at the market.

THE TOOLS

Mixing pizza or pasta dough requires nothing more exotic than a bowl, a spoon, a pair of scrupulously clean hands, and a flat work surface. If you have a standing mixer with a dough hook or a food processor, you can certainly use them to mix the dough. Pizza dough is best shaped with a pair of hands, since the best crusts are stretched into shape. Don't feel obligated to toss it into the air if you think it would just wind up on the floor, but it can be fun to flip it around. Pasta dough can simply be rolled out with a rolling pin, and then cut with a sharp knife, though a pasta machine makes it much easier to roll the dough into sheets. If there is a cutting attachment, it will make cutting the dough a snap, but you can always cut it in a shape or size that suits your recipe.

The only equipment required for cooking pasta is a pot large enough to hold a gallon of water for every pound you will be cooking. Once the water is in the pot, there should be several inches of "head space" so that the pot won't boil over. A colander is important too, since you should drain away as much cooking water as possible. Excess water will make the pasta seem softer, and will also dilute the flavor of the sauce.

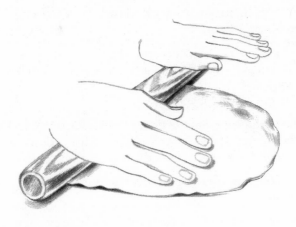

Basic Pasta Dough

This recipe will make enough fresh pasta for six entrée-sized servings. Though old customs have started to change, Italians traditionally served pasta in smaller portions, as a course preceding the roast or other meat, and seldom as an entrée.

Directions for shaping various filled pastas can be found in the other recipes in this chapter.

Makes 1½ pounds

2⅓ cups semolina, durum, or manitoba flour
2 cups all-purpose flour
½ teaspoon salt
3 whole eggs
1 to 2 tablespoons water (or as needed)

1. Combine the flours and salt in a mixing bowl. Stir to distribute the salt evenly.

2. Beat the eggs lightly in a separate bowl. Pour the eggs into the center of the bowl of flour.

3. Using a fork, gradually incorporate the flour into the eggs. Continue until the dough forms a heavy, shaggy mass. If the dough is too dry, sprinkle it with water, a teaspoon at a time, adding more only if necessary to make it workable.

4. Turn the dough out onto a floured work surface and knead it, sprinkling the dough and the work surface with additional flour as needed, until the dough has a smooth, firm, elastic consistency.

5. Wrap the dough in plastic and allow it to rest in the refrigerator for at least one hour.

6. Break off a piece of dough about the size of a large egg. Using a pasta machine or a rolling pin, roll the dough into thin sheets. Allow the dough to dry slightly, just until it does not feel tacky when touched. It should not be allowed to become brittle. Finally, cut or shape the pasta as desired.

Pasta dough can also be quickly mixed in a food processor. Place the flour and salt in the bowl of the food processor and pulse on and off until just blended. Add the lightly beaten eggs and process just until the dough has a fine, mealy consistency. If the dough forms a ball that rides on top of the blade, it is too moist. Sprinkle with additional flour and process again briefly. If the dough will not adhere when pressed together, it is too dry. Sprinkle with a teaspoon of water, and process again briefly. Turn the dough out of the food processor and press it together to form a ball. Let the dough rest before rolling, cutting, and shaping (see step 6 above).

Finely chopped fresh herbs (¼ cup), cracked peppercorns (2 tablespoons), or minced lemon zest (1 tablespoon) can be added to the dough as it is mixed to give the finished pasta a special flavor or color. You might also add a few spoonfuls of tomato paste or pureed squash, pumpkin, or spinach to the eggs before adding them to the flour. Note that, when adding any moist flavoring you may need to increase the amount of flour in order to produce the correct consistency in the dough.

Fresh pasta should be cooked as soon as possible after it is cut. It can be stored up to 24 hours in the refrigerator on flat trays covered with plastic wrap. Or make nests of the cut pasta, place them on a sheet tray and freeze until firm, then transfer the frozen pasta to freezer bags or a container. Use the frozen pasta within 4 to 6 weeks.

SERVING SUGGESTIONS

• Fresh pasta can be cut into thin or thick ribbons, either on the machine or by rolling the dough up and then cutting it with a knife.

• Light vegetable-based coulis, olive oil and garlic, or fresh herbs and a sprinkling of grated Parmesan all make excellent sauces for fresh pasta.

• Fresh pasta dough is used in the following recipes in this chapter: Chorizo-filled Ravioli with Tomato-Basil Coulis, Shrimp and Herb Tortellini with Fennel Sauce, Spinach and Chevre Cheese Agnolotti with Pesto Cream Sauce and Summer Squash, and Farfalle with Mushrooms, Basil, and Almonds.

Nutritional information, per 4-ounce serving: 340 calories; 13 grams protein; 6 grams fat; 59 grams carbohydrate; 240 milligrams sodium; 228 milligrams cholesterol.

Chorizo-filled Ravioli with Tomato-Basil Coulis

The assertive flavors of this filled pasta give you two serving options: you can pair it with a robust sauce, or you could serve it with nothing more than a dusting of freshly grated Parmesan cheese.

Makes 8 appetizer or 4 entrée servings

3 ounces chorizo sausage, chilled
2 tablespoons cooked rice, chilled
1 teaspoon jalapeño chilies, minced
2 cloves garlic, finely minced
1 teaspoon chopped fresh oregano leaves
½ teaspoon cider vinegar
½ teaspoon mild chili powder
¼ teaspoon salt (or to taste)
⅛ teaspoon cayenne pepper
⅓ recipe (about ½ pound) Basic Pasta Dough (see page 66)
2 tablespoons extra-virgin olive oil
2 plum tomatoes, peeled, seeded, and chopped
2 to 3 tablespoons chopped fresh basil leaves

1.   Grind the chorizo and rice in a food processor until fairly smooth. Add the jalapeño, garlic, oregano, vinegar, chili powder, salt, and cayenne. Continue to process just until these ingredients are thoroughly mixed.

2.   To make the ravioli, roll the pasta dough into thin sheets and cut them into 3-inch squares. Place a teaspoon of the filling on one square of pasta, and brush the edges of the square very lightly with plain water. Top with a second square and press the edges firmly to seal. If necessary or desired, use a fork to crimp the edges closed. Continue this procedure until all of the pasta squares have been filled, sealed, and crimped.

3. Bring about 2 quarts of water to a simmer and add salt to taste. Add the ravioli and cook them for about 5 minutes, then remove them with a slotted spoon and set them aside.

4. Make the coulis as follows: Heat the olive oil in a sauté pan, then add the chopped tomatoes and sauté them until they are very hot. Add the chopped basil leaves.

5. Toss the ravioli with the tomato-basil coulis and serve at once.

PREPARATION NOTES

Very finely diced roasted green or red peppers may be folded into the chorizo filling after it has been mixed in the food processor.

The ravioli may be cooked up to 3 hours in advance. Once cooked, rinse them in cold water long enough to stop the cooking and cool the ravioli. Lay them flat on a dish, then cover and refrigerate. They can be briefly reheated in a little simmering water when you are ready to serve them.

SERVING SUGGESTIONS

Instead of the tomato-and-basil coulis suggested above, serve the ravioli on a bed of salsa made from chopped tomatoes, tomatillos, bell peppers, scallions, and corn kernels for a "southwestern" look and taste.

Nutritional information, per (an entrée-sized) serving: 275 calories; 11 grams protein; 12 grams fat; 32 grams carbohydrate; 335 milligrams sodium; 150 milligrams cholesterol.

Shrimp and Herb Tortellini with Fennel Sauce

The shrimp broth that serves as the foundation of the delicate fennel sauce is easily prepared with the reserved shrimp shells and fennel tops.

Makes 4 appetizer or 2 entrée servings

4 ounces medium shrimp, peeled, deveined, and thinly sliced, shells reserved
1 tablespoon heavy cream, chilled
1 teaspoon freshly squeezed lemon juice
1 tablespoon fresh basil, chives, dill, or parsley, chopped
¼ teaspoon salt (or to taste)
¼ recipe (about ⅓ pound) Basic Pasta Dough (see page 66)
½ cup shrimp stock
1 clove garlic, finely minced
¾ cup julienned leeks, white portion only
1 cup julienned fennel
½ cup julienned carrots
4 teaspoons evaporated skim milk
1 teaspoon Pernod (optional)

IN ADVANCE   Make a stock from the shrimp shells as follows: Heat a teaspoon of olive oil in a small sauté pan, add the shells, one or two sliced mushrooms, the fennel tops, and a little sliced leek. Sauté this mixture until the shells turn a bright color. Add 2 tablespoons of dry white wine and enough water to barely cover. Reduce the heat to low and simmer for about 15 minutes. Strain this broth and set aside.

1.   Store the shrimp in the refrigerator until they are well-chilled. Combine the shrimp with the heavy cream and lemon juice and purée in a food processor until a coarse paste forms. Do not overprocess. Remove the puree to a bowl and fold in the chopped herbs and salt.

2. To make the tortellini, roll the pasta dough into thin sheets and cut into 3-inch circles. Place a spoonful of the shrimp mixture on the circles, then brush the rim of the circle lightly with water. Fold the pasta circles in half and press the edges tightly to form a seal. Overlap the two points of the half-circle to form the tortellini. Keep the tortellini refrigerated until you are ready to cook them.

3. Combine the shrimp stock with the garlic, leeks, and fennel. Simmer until the fennel is very tender, then remove from the heat and puree in a blender or with an immersion blender until smooth. Strain the puree to remove all fibers.

4. Combine the stock-and-fennel puree with the carrots, evaporated milk, and the Pernod (if desired).

5. While cooking the tortellini, warm the sauce gently over low heat. Bring about 2 quarts of water to a simmer and add salt to taste. Add the tortellini and cook for about 5 minutes, then remove them with a slotted spoon.

6. Pool the sauce in heated pasta bowls and add the tortellini.

PREPARATION NOTES

Both the sauce and the tortellini can be prepared several hours in advance. The tortellini may be cooked, drained, and then rinsed in cold water to halt the cooking. Drain once more, lay them flat, then cover and refrigerate until needed.

Prepare the sauce as explained in step 3, then chill. When you are ready to serve the tortellini, reheat the sauce and add the carrots, evaporated milk, and Pernod.

SERVING SUGGESTIONS

To give the sauce additional texture and color, finely dice additional leeks and fennel to add along with the carrots. The vegetables should be so finely cut that they will become tender by simmering in the sauce for only a minute or two.

Nutritional information, per appetizer serving: 195 calories; 12 grams protein; 4 grams fat; 30 grams carbohydrate; 205 milligrams sodium; 110 milligrams cholesterol.

Fettuccine with Puttanesca Sauce

Based on a recipe that originated in the slums of Naples, there is nothing demur about this pasta dish. Even its name—which translates as "in the style of a prostitute"—borders on the ribald. The combination of salty, spicy, and savory ingredients in a quickly prepared sauce is now popular throughout Italy.

Makes 4 entrée servings

¼ cup olive oil
2 anchovy fillets, finely chopped
4 garlic cloves, finely minced
¼ teaspoon crushed red pepper flakes
5 plum tomatoes, peeled, seeded, and chopped
¼ cup chopped fresh parsley leaves
¼ cup calamata olives, pitted and chopped
2 tablespoons capers, chopped
⅛ teaspoon salt (or to taste)
1 pound dried fettucini

IN ADVANCE To help keep the pasta hot while serving, heat a large shallow bowl by rinsing it well in hot water.

1. In a sauté pan, heat the olive oil over medium heat. Add the anchovies, garlic, and red pepper flakes. Sauté, stirring frequently, until the anchovies are lightly browned.

2. Add the tomatoes, parsley, olives, and capers and simmer until heated through. Add salt if desired.

3. In a large pot of boiling salted water, cook the fettucini according to the package directions until *al dente,* tender but still firm to the bite. Drain the pasta and place it into a heated bowl.

4. Pour the sauce over the pasta and toss to coat evenly. Serve at once.

Because several of the ingredients used in this sauce are quite high in sodium, be sure to taste the sauce before adding any extra salt. The amount of red pepper flakes can also be adjusted to suit individual taste.

While fresh fettucini can be used with this recipe, a good-quality dried pasta may have the additional "bite" that stands up to a robust sauce such as this one.

SERVING SUGGESTIONS

This dish would make an excellent centerpiece for a vegetarian menu. Add a salad made from a variety of fresh ingredients, and serve with a loaf of whole-grain bread.

Nutritional information, per entrée serving: 380 calories; 9 grams protein; 18 grams fat; 48 grams carbohydrate; 315 milligrams sodium; less than 5 milligrams cholesterol.

Pasta with Spring Vegetables

You may know this dish as "Pasta Primavera." Choose the most tender vegetables available—tiny artichokes, new peas, green onions, or slender asparagus—to concoct your own variations on this springtime favorite.

Makes 4 entrée or 6 to 8 appetizer servings

2 to 3 tablespoons *extra-virgin olive oil*
1 *garlic clove, finely minced*
2 *tablespoons finely minced shallots*
1 *zucchini, julienned*
1 *cup broccoli florets, blanched*
1 *cup cauliflower florets, blanched*
½ *cup snow peas*
½ *cup green peas, fresh or frozen*
2 to 3 *tablespoons chopped fresh herbs (chives, chervil, tarragon, basil, and/or parsley)*
⅓ *cup chicken broth or water*
¾ *pound dried linguini*
¼ *cup freshly grated Parmesan cheese*
½ *teaspoon salt*
freshly ground black pepper to taste

IN ADVANCE   While the pasta is cooking, heat a large shallow bowl by rinsing it in very hot water.

1.   Heat the olive oil in a large skillet over high heat. Add the garlic, shallots, and zucchini. Reduce the heat to medium and stir to coat all ingredients thoroughly with the olive oil. Sauté, stirring from time to time, until the zucchini is limp, for about 5 minutes.

2.   Add the broccoli and cauliflower florets, snow peas, green peas, and fresh herbs. Add the broth or water, cover the pan, and steam the vegetables briefly, until they are heated through.

3.   In a large pot of boiling salted water, cook the linguini according to the package directions until *al dente,* tender but still firm to the bite. Drain the pasta and place it in a heated bowl. Add the steamed vegetables, Parmesan, salt, and pepper. Toss to coat evenly and serve at once.

PREPARATION NOTES

Fresh shrimp could be added to this dish. Figure on about 2 ounces of shrimp per person for an entrée, or 1 ounce for an appetizer. Peel and devein the shrimp, and add them along with the broth in step 2.

SERVING SUGGESTIONS

Serve freshly grated Parmesan on the side.

Nutritional information, per serving: 400 calories; 14 grams protein; 14 grams fat; 60 grams carbohydrate; 380 milligrams sodium; 5 milligrams cholesterol.

Farfalle with Mushrooms, Basil, and Almonds

Farfalle is a butterfly- or bowtie-shaped pasta. You can use a dried pasta, but you can easily make farfalle from fresh pasta. Roll the dough into sheets, then cut them into 2-inch squares. Pinch each square in the center to make a butterfly.

Makes 8 appetizer or 4 entrée servings

2 to 3 tablespoons extra-virgin olive oil
1 tablespoon shallots, finely minced
1 garlic clove, finely minced
½ pound wild or domestic mushrooms, thinly sliced (see notes below)
2 plum tomatoes, peeled, seeded, and chopped
12 ounces farfalle, cooked and drained
¼ cup finely chopped fresh basil
¼ cup freshly grated Parmesan cheese
2 tablespoons slivered almonds, toasted

1. Heat the olive oil in a skillet over medium heat. Add the shallots and garlic and sauté, stirring from time to time, until the shallots are translucent, for about 3 minutes.

2. Increase the heat to high and add the mushrooms. Sauté, stirring occasionally, until the liquid released by the mushrooms has cooked away.

3. Add the tomatoes to the mixture and toss or stir until they are very hot.

4. Add the farfalle to the pan and toss until the pasta is well-heated. It may be necessary to add a spoonful or two of water to moisten the mixture.

5. Add the basil, Parmesan, and almonds. Toss or stir gently until the farfalle is well-coated with the herbs and cheese. Serve at once in heated pasta bowls.

To prepare pasta in advance, cook it in plenty of boiling salted water, then drain in a colander. Rinse in plenty of cold water until the pasta feels cold to the touch. Then, to keep it from sticking together, rub a little olive oil through the pasta, coating each piece.

If wild mushrooms are unavailable, use domestic mushrooms. The taste of wild mushrooms can also be introduced by rehydrating dried wild mushrooms such as cèpes, boletus, or morels, and then slicing and adding them to the dish along with domestic mushrooms.

SERVING SUGGESTIONS

This dish could also be served as a cold pasta salad. Just add a few tablespoons of a balsamic vinegar and olive oil dressing.

Nutritional information, per serving: 290 calories; 9 grams protein; 14 grams fat; 33 grams carbohydrate; 105 milligrams sodium; 5 milligrams cholesterol.

Spinach and Chèvre Cheese Agnolotti with Pesto Cream Sauce and Summer Squash

Agnolotti is one of the many different types of filled pastas found in Italian cuisine. This particular shape, a square filled pasta with ruffled edges, originated in the Piedmont region. It was traditionally prepared on Monday as a way to use up any meat left over from Sunday dinner.

Makes 4 appetizer or 2 entrée servings

1 tablespoon extra-virgin olive oil
2 teaspoons shallot, finely minced
⅓ cup cooked spinach, chopped
2 ounces chèvre cheese
¼ cup part-skim ricotta cheese
1 egg white, lightly beaten
2 tablespoons freshly grated Parmesan cheese
¼ recipe (about ⅓ pound) Basic Pasta Dough (see page 66)
2 tablespoons finely chopped basil
2 teaspoons pine nuts, toasted
¼ teaspoons finely minced garlic
3 tablespoons heavy cream
2 small yellow summer squash or zucchini, julienned

1. In a small sauté pan, heat about ½ teaspoon of the olive oil over medium heat. Add the shallot and spinach and sauté until the mixture is fairly dry. Remove the spinach mixture from the pan and place it in a mixing bowl. Allow it to cool to room temperature.

2. Blend the chèvre, ricotta, egg white, and half of the Parmesan with the spinach. Refrigerate until well-chilled.

3. To make the agnolotti, roll out the pasta dough into thin sheets and cut into 3-inch squares. Place a spoonful of the spinach mixture on each square, and brush the edges lightly with water. Fold the pasta squares in half to form a triangle, then press the edges tightly to form a seal. Overlap the two points of the triangle to form the agnolotti. Continue this procedure until all of the pasta squares have been filled, sealed, and crimped. Keep the agnolotti refrigerated until you are ready to cook them.

4. To prepare the pesto cream, combine the remaining olive oil in a blender with the basil, pine nuts, garlic, and the remaining Parmesan. Blend until smooth. With the blender running, add the heavy cream and process until thoroughly combined. Reserve until needed.

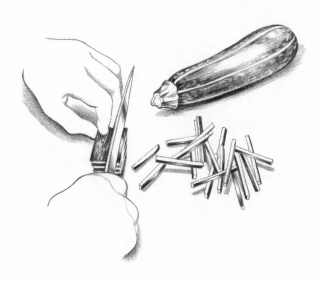

5. Bring about 2 quarts of water to a simmer and add salt to taste. Add the agnolotti and cook them for about 5 minutes, then remove them with a slotted spoon and set aside.

6. Drop the summer squash into the water that was used to cook the agnolotti and simmer for about 1 minute. Drain through a colander, cover, and keep warm while finishing the agnolotti.

7. In the pot that was used to cook the agnolotti and the summer squash, heat the pesto cream sauce over medium heat. When the cream is hot, add the agnolotti. Toss gently to coat with the sauce and to heat through.

8. Serve the hot agnolotti with the squash.

PREPARATION NOTES

While this dish may seem a little complicated, it is relatively simple to prepare in advance. The uncooked agnolotti can be refrigerated for up to 24 hours before cooking. They can be cooked up to three hours before serving. The pesto cream sauce can be refrigerated for up to two days.

The agnolotti and the pesto cream sauce can then be tossed together just before serving and reheated either in a microwave or on the stovetop.

SERVING SUGGESTIONS

• For a colorful effect, use a combination of yellow squash and zucchini. Cut the skin away in ¼-inch-thick slices, then cut this brightly colored skin into matchstick-sized strips and steam briefly before adding them to the sauce. Make a "nest" for the agnolotti with this mixture.

• Other vegetables, including finely julienned carrots, leeks, green beans, or strips of roasted peppers, can also be added to make this dish more substantial.

Nutritional information, per entrée-sized serving: 285 calories; 12 grams protein; 15 grams fat; 28 grams carbohydrate; 260 milligrams sodium; 105 milligrams cholesterol.

Pizza

Pizza from a good pizzeria has a crisp crust that isn't doughy in the center, and is topped with enough ingredients to give punch to every bite. Pizzerias are equipped with special ovens to give the finished pizza the perfect crust; some even have wood-fired ovens. St. Andrew's Cafe, a restaurant on the campus of The Culinary Institute of America, features pizzas from its wood-fired oven in both appetizer- and entrée-sized servings. You can get excellent results in a home oven by using a pizza stone, which is a ceramic platter that holds the pizza as it bakes. You can also line an oven rack with ceramic tiles, which can be found in building supply stores. There are also special pizza pans you can try that are perforated with holes. Although an oven needs to be quite hot to make a good pizza, you don't absolutely need to preheat the oven. Just put the pizza into a cold oven, then set it to the temperature stated in the recipe.

Basic Pizza Dough

The success of any pizza rests squarely on the quality of the dough, since at its heart, pizza is simply a special type of bread. This dough can be baked in pans to create a thicker, chewier Sicilian-style pizza, or stretched thin and baked either on a pizza stone or directly on the floor of the oven for a crisper crust.

Makes enough for 4 individual pizzas or 1 large pizza

1 teaspoon honey
¾ cup warm water
1 package dry yeast
1⅓ cups bread flour
1 cup semolina flour
¼ teaspoon salt
vegetable oil as needed
cornmeal as needed

1. Combine the honey, ¼ cup of the water, and the yeast. Stir in enough of the bread flour to make a thin batter with the consistency of buttermilk. Cover and let rise in a warm spot for about 1 hour.

2. Add the remaining bread flour and the semolina to the batter, and then knead in a mixer with a dough hook or by hand until the dough is smooth, springy, and elastic. Rub it lightly with oil, place in a clean bowl, and cover with a cloth. Let the dough rise until it doubles in volume, for about 2 to 3 hours.

3. Punch down the dough, and divide it into four equal pieces for individual pizzas or leave whole for one large pizza. Round the dough into smooth balls, cover, and let rise once more until they double in volume, for about 1 hour.

4. Flatten the balls of dough and roll or stretch until they are about ⅓-inch thick. Place the dough on baking sheets sprinkled with cornmeal. The pizza dough can either be refrigerated until needed or topped and baked.

PREPARATION NOTES

This pizza dough recipe can easily be doubled. Any dough that will not be used immediately can be frozen for later use.

To make whole wheat pizza dough, substitute one-third to one-half of the bread flour with whole wheat flour.

SERVING SUGGESTIONS

• In addition to pizza, this dough can also be used to prepare a delicious grilled bread. Shape the dough as you would for individual pizzas, then grill it over hot coals for about 2 minutes on each side until blistered and browned. After the first side is cooked, drizzle it with olive oil and scatter it with fresh herbs such as oregano, basil, thyme, or rosemary.

• This dough can also be used to prepare pita bread: Mix, shape, and flatten the dough into individual pizzas (see steps 2 through 4). Heat the oven to 500°F and bake the pitas for about 10 minutes. They will puff up during baking and then deflate when removed from the oven, creating the "pocket."

Nutritional information, per individual pizza: 230 calories; 7 grams protein; 2 grams fat; 45 grams carbohydrate; 155 milligrams sodium; 0 milligrams cholesterol.

Pizza with Mozzarella and Roasted Tomatoes

Roasting gives tomatoes a wonderful flavor and helps to cook away some of the moisture that might otherwise leave you with a soggy crust. If good-quality fresh tomatoes aren't available, substitute sun-dried tomatoes.

Makes 4 servings

1 recipe Basic Pizza Dough (see page 82), shaped as desired
1 tablespoon extra-virgin olive oil
1 tablespoon fresh basil leaves, chopped
1 teaspoon fresh oregano leaves, chopped
1 garlic clove, finely minced
cracked black peppercorns to taste
1 cup tomato puree
4 plum tomatoes, sliced and roasted
4¼ ounces part-skim mozzarella, sliced thin
4 tablespoons freshly grated Parmesan cheese

IN ADVANCE To roast the tomatoes, slice them thickly and place in a single layer on a baking sheet. Bake in a 375°F oven for 20 to 25 minutes.

1. Remove the pizza dough from the refrigerator and allow it to return to room temperature. Let rise for several minutes.

2. Blend the olive oil, basil, oregano, garlic, and cracked pepper. Spread this mixture evenly over the pizza dough.

3. Spread the pizza with the tomato puree and top with the roasted tomatoes and mozzarella. Sprinkle with Parmesan cheese.

4. Place the pizza on a baking sheet and bake in a 475°F oven until the dough is golden and crisp, about 8 to 10 minutes.

5. Serve while still very hot.

PREPARATION NOTES

To make slicing easier, put the mozzarella in the freezer for 15 minutes. Then store the sliced cheese in the freezer while assembling the other ingredients.

SERVING SUGGESTIONS

Other cheeses can be substituted for mozzarella. Monterey Jack cheese—plain or with peppers—or provolone are both good choices.

Nutritional information (based on part-skim mozzarella; other cheeses would modify the analysis), per serving: 460 calories; 18 grams protein; 19 grams fat; 57 grams carbohydrate; 500 milligrams sodium; 20 milligrams cholesterol.

St. Andrew's Vegetable Pizza

At the height of the summer, when the produce stands and farmer's markets are full of wonderful vegetables and herbs, feel free to select your favorite vegetables for this pizza.

Makes 4 servings

1 recipe Basic Pizza Dough (see page 82), shaped as desired
1 teaspoon olive oil
1 garlic clove, finely minced
1 cup julienned red pepper
½ cup julienned red onion
1 tablespoon broth or water
1 cup peeled, seeded, and chopped tomato
2 tablespoons vinaigrette (see Chapter 1 pages 4–9)
¾ cup thinly sliced yellow squash or zucchini
¾ cup thinly sliced eggplant
½ cup thinly sliced mushrooms (wild or domestic)
¼ teaspoon cracked black peppercorns
2 ounces fresh goat cheese, crumbled

1. Remove the pizza dough from the refrigerator and allow it to return to room temperature. Let rise for several minutes.

2. In a sauté pan, heat the olive oil over medium heat. Add the garlic and sauté for about 1 minute. Add the red pepper, red onion, and the broth or water. Continue to sauté over medium heat, stirring occasionally, for about 3 minutes, or until the red peppers are limp.

3. Add the chopped tomato and continue to sauté until the mixture is heated through. Remove from the heat and allow to cool briefly.

4. Combine the vinaigrette with the sliced vegetables and cracked peppercorns.

5. Spread the onion, pepper, and tomato mixture on the pizza dough and top with the vegetables. Sprinkle with the crumbled goat cheese.

6.   Place the pizza on a baking sheet and bake in a 475°F oven until the dough is golden and crisp, about 8 to 10 minutes.

7.   Serve while still very hot.

PREPARATION NOTES

If you decide to experiment with other vegetables, follow these basic guidelines: Dense vegetables (such as carrots, parsnips, broccoli, cauliflower, or squashes) should be cooked until tender before they are combined with the vinaigrette. Vegetables with a lot of natural moisture (spinach, zucchini, or tomatoes, for example) benefit from being quickly sautéed to dry them slightly.

SERVING SUGGESTIONS

The choice of ingredients for the vinaigrette can be made according to your personal taste. Add fresh herbs, chopped olives, capers, additional garlic, or whatever you feel will enhance the overall flavor impact of the dish.

Nutritional information, per serving: 460 calories; 18 grams protein; 18 grams fat; 57 grams carbohydrate; 500 milligrams sodium; 20 milligrams cholesterol.

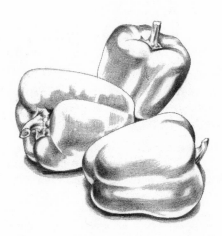

Wild Mushroom and Artichoke Pizza

Wild mushrooms have become increasingly available throughout the country. However, if you cannot find them, this recipe would work well made with the domestic button mushrooms found in any supermarket. In either case, be sure that the pan is thoroughly preheated before sautéing the mushrooms in step 2.

Makes 4 servings

cornmeal as needed
1 recipe Basic Pizza Dough (see page 82), shaped as desired
2 tablespoons extra-virgin olive oil
2 to 3 cloves garlic, minced fine
2 cups wild mushrooms, sliced
1 teaspoon chopped fresh thyme leaves (or ½ teaspoon dried)
½ cup quartered artichoke bottoms, cooked until tender
½ teaspoon salt
¼ teaspoon pepper
½ cup mozzarella cheese, grated

IN ADVANCE   Preheat the oven to 425°F.

1.   Scatter the cornmeal on a baking sheet, then set the shaped pizza in the center. Allow the dough to return to room temperature and to rise for several minutes.

2.   Heat 1 tablespoon of the olive oil in a sauté pan over high heat. Add the garlic and mushrooms and sauté, stirring from time to time, until the mushrooms are lightly browned, for about 3 to 4 minutes.

3.   Drizzle the remaining oil over the pizza dough, and scatter the thyme leaves evenly over the surface. Top with the sautéed mushrooms, artichoke bottoms, salt, pepper, and grated cheese.

4. Bake the pizza in the preheated oven for about 10 minutes, or until the dough is golden and crisp.

5. Serve the pizza while it is still very hot.

PREPARATION NOTES

This recipe can be prepared with either one or a combination of different mushrooms. Be aware of each type's preparation requirements. Mushrooms such as shiitakes have tough stems that should be removed. Chanterelles, morels, and oak mushrooms need only a trimming on the stem end. If possible, try brushing away dirt rather than rinsing the mushrooms. They tend to absorb water easily, which could make the finished pizza soggy.

Use fresh artichokes, or artichoke bottoms packed in brine. Or, if you prefer, you could use marinated artichoke hearts in this recipe. Be sure that they are sliced or quartered so that it is not a challenge to eat the pizza.

SERVING SUGGESTIONS

• This would make an excellent first course for Roast Loin of Pork with Honey and Mustard Glaze (see page 142) or Grilled Chicken with Fennel (see page 114).

• Make this pizza the centerpiece of a meal, and accompany with a salad of field greens garnished with a selection of raw or lightly steamed vegetables dressed with Roasted Garlic and Mustard Vinaigrette (see page 4).

Nutritional information, per serving: 360 calories; 14 grams protein; 12 grams fat; 56 grams carbohydrate; 420 milligrams sodium; 10 milligrams cholesterol.

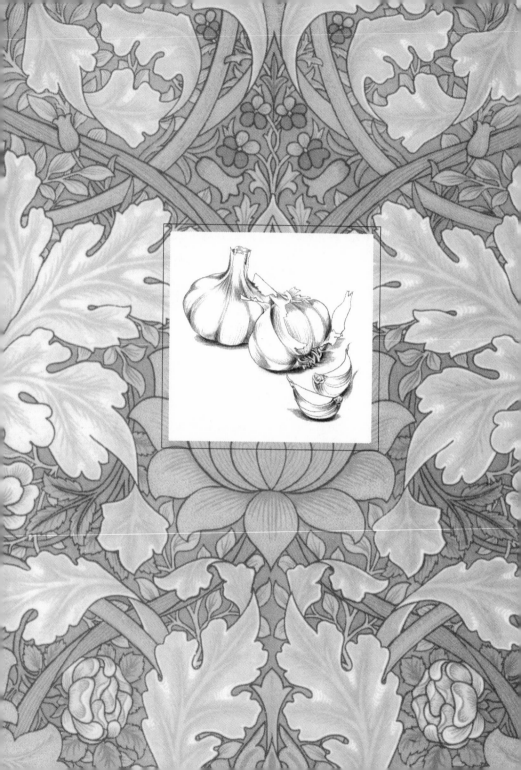

Entrées

Entrée is a French word that translates literally as "beginning, debut, or introduction." In another era, when meals were more elaborate and formal than they are now, menus had many more courses than we are familiar with, or comfortable preparing, serving, or eating on a daily basis. Consider, as an example, a menu for a dinner party for twenty, served in 1882 by the grandmother of the Countess of Toulouse-Lautrec: *Potages* (soups) were served first—a consommé and a bisque. Next came the *relevés,* a course similar to our appetizer; it included turbot with oyster sauce and beef tenderloin with a Richelieu sauce. What were then referred to as *entrées* followed: individual meat timbales, duck livers *à la Toulousaine,* and an aspic of game birds. A tea sorbet preceded the *rôtis* (roasts), an offering of truffled turkey and roast pheasants along with two vegetable dishes, known as the *entremets.* After that, finally, came dessert: apricot nougat, cold pinapple soufflés, and a cake.

Our contemporary menus are significantly simpler, reduced from six courses to an average of three or four for an elegant affair or holiday feast. The entrée, which was originally just a "start," has now become the main event. The forces behind these changes are many, and include a concern for health and fitness, and the increased need to balance family life and work.

When we do take the time to create a special meal for our family and friends, we tend to plan the meal around the entrée. For example, an entrée of poached fish may call for an opening dish that has some interesting flavor and texture; this dish may include richer ingredients to highlight the lightness of the fish. On the other hand, if the entrée's preparation is complicated, its appetizer should be a very simple dish that can be prepared quickly, or well in advance, or even purchased already prepared.

Side dishes, too, should be chosen to complement the entrée. A rich, slowly simmered stew is enhanced by light noodles or savory dumplings that absorb its delicious sauce. Quickly grilled or broiled foods can meet the challenges of the smoky robust flavors of roasted vegetables. Or, rather than subtly complementing the flavors and textures of the main dish, you might prefer a side dish that provides a contrast of color and texture.

The recipes in this chapter are built around foods that are normally available in large supermarkets. To make shopping easier, substitutes have been suggested in many instances. Since meat, fish, and poultry tend to be the most expensive elements of a meal, make sure that you are getting the best quality for your money. Foods that will be quickly sautéed, grilled, steamed, or shallow-poached should be selected from among the more tender cuts: Beef steaks cut from the tenderloin or rib; veal cutlets from the top round; chicken or duck breasts; chops of pork or veal from the rib or loin; the tenderloin of pork; fish that has been pan-dressed, filleted, or cut into steaks.

Baked, braised, or stewed entrées can often accommodate the longer, slower cooking times necessary to bring out the best of more mature or well-exercised cuts of meat (chuck steaks, brisket, shanks, and so on), stewing hens, or turkey legs.

New England Shore Dinner

This dish requires no additional courses, especially if a good quantity of seasonal vegetables are introduced in addition to those listed below. Add parcooked slices or chunks of carrots, zucchini, and halved leeks, or other vegetables that might be in season.

Makes 4 servings

1 tablespoon unsalted butter
1 garlic clove, finely minced
1 small onion, finely minced
1½ cups broth (fish, chicken, or vegetable)
1 whole bay leaf
1 sprig fresh thyme
3 to 4 whole black peppercorns
2 ears of corn, shucked and halved
4 small red bliss potatoes, cooked
8 boiling onions, peeled and steamed
2 lobster tails, split lengthwise
4 pieces of scrod fillet (2 ounces each)
8 mussels, scrubbed and debearded

1. Heat the butter in a large pot. Add the garlic and onion and sauté them until the onion is limp.

2. Add the broth, bay leaf, thyme, and peppercorns and bring the mixture to a simmer.

3. Layer the remaining ingredients in a steamer insert: Place the corn, potatoes, boiling onions, and lobster tails in the first layer, then top with the scrod and mussels. If using a tiered bamboo or aluminum steamer basket, place the ingredients in separate "tiers."

4. Place the steamer insert over the simmering broth, cover the pan tightly, and steam for about 20 minutes over low heat.

5. Remove the cover and serve the vegetables, fish, and shellfish with a cup of the flavorful broth.

PREPARATION NOTES

If you do not have either a steamer insert or a tiered steamer, you can use a colander inside a pot large enough to accommodate it. A lid can be created by covering the pot with aluminum foil.

SERVING SUGGESTIONS

Try serving the dinner directly from the steamer, allowing guests to help themselves. Other ingredients may be added to make this a more elaborate or substantial feast. For a more intensely flavored dish, replace the scrod with small portions of tuna, shark, or swordfish.

Nutritional information per serving: 270 calories; 30 grams protein; 6 grams fat; 22 grams carbohydrate; 195 milligrams sodium; 120 milligrams cholesterol.

Catfish Topped with Crabmeat and Cornbread Crumbs

Farm-raised catfish, which has a firm texture and sweet taste, is readily available in most supermarkets or fish stores year-round.

Makes 4 servings

2 teaspoons unsalted butter
¼ cup finely minced onion
3 tablespoons heavy cream
3 ounces crabmeat, picked to remove shells or cartilage
¼ teaspoon salt (or to taste)
freshly ground pepper to taste
4 catfish fillets (about 4 to 5 ounces each)
½ cup cornbread crumbs
¼ cup dry white wine
½ cup fish or vegetable broth
¼ cup julienned cured ham
2 tablespoons dry sherry

IN ADVANCE Preheat the oven to 350°F. Lightly butter an 8-inch square baking dish.

1. Heat the butter in a skillet. Add the onions and sauté over medium heat until they are limp. Add half of the heavy cream and simmer, stirring occasionally until thickened. Remove the pan from the heat.

2. Fold the crabmeat into the onions and cream, then add the salt and pepper. Top each fillet with one-fourth of the mixture and spread it into an even layer. Sprinkle with an even layer of cornbread crumbs. Place the fillets in a lightly buttered baking dish and set aside.

3. Bring the wine and broth to a simmer and add them to the baking dish carefully, taking care not to moisten the cornbread topping. Place the dish in a 350°F oven and bake for about 12 minutes, or until the catfish is properly cooked and the cornbread crumbs have formed a crisp crust.

4. While the fish is cooking, simmer the remaining heavy cream with the ham in a skillet for about 3 minutes until the cream is thickened.

5. Remove the fish to a heated serving platter or to individual plates. Add the cooking liquid from the baking dish to the cream and ham mixture and simmer for another 2 to 3 minutes, or until the sauce is lightly thickened. Add the dry sherry, then season to taste with salt and pepper.

6. Ladle the hot sauce around the fish and serve at once.

PREPARATION NOTES

This dish can be completely assembled—ready to pop into the oven—up to 2 hours in advance, which makes it a good choice for entertaining. Bake and serve in a handsome casserole.

Monkfish, grouper, or orange roughy can be substituted for the catfish if you prefer.

SERVING SUGGESTIONS

• Spinach or escarole that has been sautéed with garlic would be a good accompaniment, and simple to prepare.

• For a "down-home" southern flavor, try okra stewed with tomatoes, or a spicy Ratatouille (see page 198).

Nutritional information per serving: 250 calories; 26 grams protein; 13 grams fat; 7 grams carbohydrate; 560 milligrams sodium; 120 milligrams cholesterol.

Cioppino

If you surveyed cooks from southern France and Italy for the definitive recipe for *cioppino* or *bouillabaisse,* you would likely get as many answers as the number of people you asked. These delicious seafood-based stews, simmered in a garlicky tomato broth, are made with fresh, locally available fish that are caught the same day. Ask your fish vendor to suggest other varieties for your own version, or to substitute for items suggested here that may not be available in your area.

Makes 4 servings

1 tablespoon olive oil
½ cup finely diced onion
1 green or red pepper, julienned
½ cup julienned fennel
4 garlic cloves, finely minced
4 to 5 plum tomatoes, peeled, seeded, and diced
⅓ cup tomato puree
1 cup fish or vegetable broth
⅓ cup dry white wine
1 bay leaf
4 pieces mako shark or swordfish (about 2 to 3 ounces each)
8 large shrimp, peeled and deveined
8 cherrystone clams, thoroughly scrubbed
1 tablespoon minced fresh basil

1.   Heat the olive oil in a large skillet or soup pot. Add the onion, pepper, fennel, and garlic and sauté over medium heat until they are limp, about 4 to 5 minutes.

2.   Add the diced tomatoes and tomato puree and sauté for another 3 to 4 minutes, stirring from time to time.

3. Add the broth, wine, bay leaf, shark, shrimp, and clams. Cover the pot and "steam" the mixture until the clam shells have opened, about 5 minutes.

4. Stir the basil into the *cioppino,* then ladle it into heated soup plates to serve.

PREPARATION NOTES

For culinary purists, the choices of fish and shellfish for cioppino are often a matter of debate; in practice, however, cioppino is an excellent vehicle for preparing a variety of fish. Try adding a couple of cut-up blue crabs, replace the clams with mussels, or use tuna in place of the shark or swordfish. If you can find it in your area, you might replace the shrimp with crayfish.

SERVING SUGGESTIONS

• Throughout the Mediterranean, a red, spicy version of mayonnaise (known as *rouille*) or a garlic-infused mayonnaise (*aïoli*) would often be swirled into the cioppino, added by diners to suit their own tastes.

• To make a quick, fiery version of rouille, blend 3 or 4 tablespoons of pureed roasted red peppers, 4 to 5 finely minced garlic cloves, and a dash of cayenne into ½ cup of mayonnaise (homemade or prepared).

• For aïoli, heat 2 tablespoons of dry white wine or vermouth and add a teaspoon of saffron threads. Let them steep in the wine for about 10 minutes. Add the saffron to ½ cup of mayonnaise, along with 4 to 5 finely minced garlic cloves, salt, pepper, and lemon juice to taste.

• For a reduced-fat version of aïoli or rouille, replace the mayonnaise with pureed part-skim ricotta cheese or a non-fat or low-fat sour cream substitute.

• Brush slices of French bread with a paste of olive oil and garlic, toast to a golden brown, and either float in the soup as large "croutons" or serve on the side.

Nutritional information per serving: 215 calories; 26 grams protein; 7 grams fat; 13 grams carbohydrate; 135 milligrams sodium; 75 milligrams cholesterol.

Broiled Red Perch with Lime-Tequila Vinaigrette

Mirin, one of the ingredients used in the vinaigrette, is a sweetened sake used in Japanese-style broiled dishes. It can usually be found in the specialty or ethnic foods sections of larger grocery stores, or in markets that specialize in Asian foodstuffs. Sweet sherry or vermouth can be substituted if mirin is not available.

Makes 4 servings

½ cup vegetable or chicken broth
1 teaspoon cornstarch or arrowroot
3 tablespoons peanut or sesame oil
2 tablespoons lime juice, freshly squeezed
1 tablespoon tequila
1 tablespoon mirin
1 tablespoon chopped fresh cilantro
¼ teaspoon salt (or to taste)
½ teaspoon cracked black peppercorns
4 red perch fillets, skin attached (about 5 ounces each)

1. To prepare the vinaigrette, bring the broth to a boil. As it heats, dilute the cornstarch in a small amount of cold broth or water. Add the diluted cornstarch to the boiling broth and stir. Remove from the heat and stir in the oil, lime juice, tequila, mirin, cilantro, salt, and pepper. Set aside.

2. Score the skin of the fish in a diamond pattern. This will help the fish to cook quickly and evenly.

3. Place the fillets, skin side down, on a baking dish or broiler plate and brush evenly with the vinaigrette. Broil for about 3 minutes, then turn the fish and brush once more with the vinaigrette. Broil for another 3 to 4 minutes, or until the fish is completely cooked.

4. Drizzle the fish with a little additional vinaigrette and serve.

PREPARATION NOTES

The vinaigrette recipe can be doubled or even tripled, and used as a marinade for chicken, fish, and vegetables. It will keep well for several days when refrigerated.

The fish may be grilled instead of broiled if preferred.

SERVING SUGGESTIONS

This dish was inspired by some of Florida's native bounty: fresh fish from both the Gulf of Mexico and the Atlantic, and wonderful citrus fruits. To give it a more interesting appearance and flavor, toss sliced yellow and red grapefruit, diced fresh tomato, and sliced avocado with a little of the remaining vinaigrette. To serve, arrange this salad on the plate with the fish.

Nutritional information per serving: 175 calories; 21 grams protein; 9 grams fat; 3 grams carbohydrate; 210 milligrams sodium; 45 milligrams cholesterol.

Roasted Monkfish with Niçoise Olives and Pernod Sauce

Monkfish is a mildly-flavored fish that has been referred to as "poor man's lobster" because of its similarty to lobster's texture. It is sold as boneless fillets, cut from the tail of a large, and rather ugly fish known to fishermen by a variety of names, including belly-fish, all-mouth, or lawyer fish. Monkfish, a less perjorative name, has been adopted by fish vendors in an effort to make this delicious fish sound as tempting as it tastes.

Makes 4 servings

1 pound monkfish, left whole
4 tablespoons lime juice, freshly squeezed
2 teaspoons green peppercorns, rinsed and mashed
1 teaspoon chopped fresh tarragon
1 teaspoon minced shallots
2 tablespoons tomato paste
1 tablespoon Pernod
¾ cup fish or vegetable stock
½ teaspoon cornstarch or arrowroot
2 tablespoons evaporated skim milk
8 Niçoise olives, pitted

1. Trim away any remaining connective tissue from the monkfish carefully, then place in a baking dish.

2. Combine the lime juice, green peppercorns, tarragon, and shallots. Pour this mixture over the monkfish, turn the fish to coat it evenly, and allow it to marinate for about 15 minutes.

3. Roast the monkfish in a 450°F oven for about 10 minutes, or until it reaches internal temperature of 145°F (use an instant reading thermometer). Remove the fish from the oven and allow it to rest while preparing the sauce.

4. Sauté the tomato paste in a small saucepan over medium heat until it takes on a rusty color and has a sweet aroma. Add the Pernod and stir well to blend.

5. Add the fish or vegetable stock and bring the sauce to a simmer.

6. Dilute the cornstarch in the milk and add it to the sauce. Let simmer until thickened (about 30 seconds), then remove from the heat and stir in the olives.

7. Slice the fish and serve it on heated plates with the sauce.

PREPARATION NOTES

Another firmly textured fish, such as catfish, mako shark, mahi-mahi, or halibut, could be substituted for the monkfish. Ask your fish vendor to suggest a fish that will stand up to both the dry heat of the roasting and the strong flavors of the marinade and the sauce.

Pernod, an anise-flavored liqueur, lends a unique flavor to this dish. If you prefer not to include it, add a teaspoon of fennel or anise seeds to the green peppercorn mixture used to coat the fish.

SERVING SUGGESTIONS

Grilled polenta or risotto would be good choices to serve with this fish.

Nutritional information, per serving: 195 calories; 20 grams protein; 4 grams fat; 6 grams carbohydrate; 350 milligrams sodium; 40 milligrams cholesterol.

Grouper Poached in Louisiana Saffron Broth

Poaching is an excellent technique for preparing lean fish. In this recipe, the fish cooks in an intensely-flavored broth. As with all correctly poached fish, the flesh should remain moist and tender, without falling apart or shredding. The trick is to cook the fish gently. Throughout the poaching process be sure to maintain only the slightest hint of movement on the surface of the broth. Turn the heat down as far as you can, or use a heat diffuser or "flame-tamer," a device found in cookware shops or the kitchen wares section of hardware stores.

Makes 4 servings

2 teaspoons olive oil
1 leek, white portion only, julienned
1 garlic clove, finely minced
¼ teaspoon red pepper flakes
½ teaspoon crushed saffron threads
1 cup julienned fennel
2 plum tomatoes, peeled, seeded, and diced
1 large piece orange rind
1 bay leaf
2½ cups fish or chicken broth (or a combination)
½ cup dry white wine
4 grouper fillets (about 4 to 5 ounces each)

1. Heat the olive oil in a large skillet. Add the leek, garlic, and red pepper flakes and sauté over low to medium heat until the leeks are quite tender, for about 5 minutes.

2. Add the saffron, fennel, tomatoes, orange rind, bay leaf, broth, and wine. Bring to a simmer and cook until the fennel is tender.

3. Add the grouper fillets and lower the heat so that the broth is barely simmering. Poach the fish for about 10 to 12 minutes, or until just cooked through.

4. Remove and discard the orange rind and bay leaf. Serve the fish in soup plates with the broth and vegetables.

PREPARATION NOTES

This dish adapts well to a variety of lean, firm-textured fish. Monkfish, tilefish (sometimes referred to as golden bass), mahi-mahi, orange roughy, and snapper are all good choices.

The broth can be prepared through step 2, cooled quickly, and refrigerated for up to 2 days. Be sure to bring the broth to a full boil before continuing with the recipe.

Use the broth to poach boneless skinless chicken breast.

SERVING SUGGESTIONS

• Boiled or steamed rice would be a good choice to serve with this dish.

• For a one-dish meal, add other seasonal vegetables to the broth as it simmers: chunks of zucchini or yellow squash, green beans, peas, asparagus tips, or shredded escarole or spinach.

Nutritional information per serving: 150 calories; 22 grams protein; 3 grams fat; 7 grams carbohydrate; 70 milligrams sodium; 40 milligrams cholesterol.

Squid in Diablo Sauce with Linguine

Squid—often sold under its Italian name, *calamari*—is a delicious seafood. While many people are afraid to cook squid, fearing that it might become rubbery or tough, as long as you are careful not to overcook it, the meat will remain tender.

Makes 4 servings

3 tablespoons olive oil
½ cup finely minced onions
2 garlic cloves, finely minced
½ teaspoon red pepper flakes
½ cup canned crushed tomatoes
3 plum tomatoes, peeled, seeded, and chopped
¼ cup tomato paste
1 bay leaf
½ pound pork neck bones, roasted or smoked
2 tablespoons chopped fresh herbs (parsley, oregano, and/or basil)
¼ teaspoon salt
freshly ground black pepper to taste
¾ pound squid, cleaned and sliced (¼-inch-thick slices)
¾ pound linguine

IN ADVANCE Roast the pork neck bones in a 375°F oven for about 30 minutes, or until they are a deep brown. This can be done well in advance, and the bones frozen for up to 3 months until you are ready to prepare the sauce.

1. Heat 1 tablespoon of the olive oil in a skillet over medium heat. Add the onion and garlic and sauté until the onion turns a light golden brown.

2. Add the red pepper flakes and sauté for an additional 1 to 2 minutes to release their flavor. Add the canned and fresh tomatoes, the tomato paste, bay leaf, and pork bones. Bring the sauce to a simmer and continue to cook, stirring from time to time, over medium heat, for about 45 minutes, or until the sauce has developed a good rich flavor.

3. Remove the sauce from the heat and discard the bay leaf and pork bones. Let cool slightly, then puree the sauce through a food mill or fine sieve.

4. Return the sauce to the skillet, add the chopped fresh herbs, salt, and pepper, and bring to a simmer over medium heat.

5. In a separate skillet, heat the remaining olive oil over high heat. Pat the squid dry with absorbent toweling, then add the pieces to the hot oil. Toss or stir the squid as it sautés, for about 1 to 2 minutes.

6. Add the sauce to the sautéed squid and simmer gently over low heat for about 15 minutes.

7. Continue to simmer the squid while cooking the linguine in plenty of boiling salted water.

8. Drain the pasta and turn it into a large heated bowl. Top the pasta with the squid and sauce, and serve at once.

PREPARATION NOTES

The sauce may be prepared through step 3, then refrigerated for up to 3 days or frozen for up to 2 months. For the best flavor, add the fresh herbs just before serving the sauce.

SERVING SUGGESTIONS

• Instead of one large pasta bowl, serve a "nest" of the hot pasta in heated individual soup plates, topped with the squid and sauce.

• Brush slices of bread with a paste of olive oil and roasted garlic, lightly toast under the broiler to a golden brown, and serve on the side.

Nutritional information, per serving: 360 calories; 21 grams protein; 12 grams fat; 43 grams carbohydrate; 565 milligrams sodium; 155 milligrams cholesterol.

Mussels and Shrimp with Fresh Tomatoes and Orzo

This recipe can be prepared from start to finish in less than 30 minutes. If you like the idea of offering finger bowls to your guests, the shrimp can be cooked in their shells; otherwise, be sure to peel the shrimp first.

Makes 4 servings

1 tablespoon olive oil
2 cloves garlic, finely minced
½ cup diced onion
1 red or green pepper, diced
¼ teaspoons crushed saffron threads
1½ cups chicken or vegetable broth
½ cup orzo
½ teaspoons salt
8 to 12 mussels, scrubbed and debearded
½ pound large shrimp (16 to 20 count)
3 ounces chorizo or other cured smoked sausage
1 cup seeded and chopped tomatoes
½ cup fresh or frozen green peas
2 scallions, sliced thinly on the bias

1. Heat the olive oil in a skillet or paella pan over medium–high heat. Add the garlic, onion, and pepper. Cook, stirring occasionally, until the onion turns a light golden brown. Add the saffron and continue to sauté the mixture for another 2 to 3 minutes, or until the saffron begins to release its color.

2. Add the broth, orzo, and salt. Stir to combine all the ingredients and bring the broth to a simmer. Cover the pan and cook over low heat for about 10 minutes.

3. Remove the cover and add the mussels, shrimp, and chorizo. Continue to simmer without stirring for another 8 to 10 minutes, or until the shrimp are fully cooked.

4. Using a fork, stir in the tomatoes and peas, then cover the pan again and cook over low heat for another 3 to 4 minutes.

5. Sprinkle with the chopped scallions and serve at once.

PREPARATION NOTES

Experiment with other shellfish in this dish: clams, lobster tails, crab legs, or oysters. Chicken legs may also be included, either in addition to or as a substitute for the seafood. Separate whole legs into drumsticks and thighs, and figure on one piece per person. Brown the chicken in the olive oil along with the onions in step 1, then continue with the recipe as indicated.

SERVING SUGGESTIONS

This is a true "one-pot" meal, and if it is prepared in a casserole it can be cooked and served in the same vessel. Serve with a loaf of good crusty French or Italian bread to mop up any juices left in the dish.

Nutritional information per serving: 275 calories; 24 grams protein; 11 grams fat; 21 grams carbohydrate; 535 milligrams sodium; 109 milligrams cholesterol.

Tandoori Morg
(Roast Chicken with Yogurt Masala)

Masala is a catchall term used to indicate a blend of spices. For the best flavor, purchase whole cumin, coriander, and cardamom seeds. Toast them over low heat in a dry skillet until they begin to release their aromas. Then grind them in a spice grinder, coffee grinder, or with a mortar and pestle.

Makes 4 to 6 servings

1 roasting chicken (about 3½ pounds)
juice of 1 lemon
2 teaspoons salt
½ teaspoon saffron threads
4 tablespoons boiling water
1 cup plain yogurt
4 garlic cloves, finely minced
2 tablespoons grated fresh ginger
1 tablespoon ground cumin seeds
1 tablespoon ground cardamom seeds
2 teaspoons ground coriander seeds
1 to 2 teaspoons cayenne pepper (or to taste)
3 tablespoons clarified butter, heated

IN ADVANCE Place whole cumin, cardamonom, and coriander seeds in a small dry skillet. Toast the seeds over medium heat, stirring or tossing constantly, until they are hot and give off a strong aroma. Let them cool slightly, and then grind with a mortar and pestle or in a coffee or spice grinder.

1. Remove the skin from the chicken, using a paring knife as necessary to cut it away. Cut the skinned chicken into eight pieces: two legs, two thighs, two breasts, and two wings. Use a sharp paring knife to score the breasts and thigh with ⅛ inch cuts. Mix the lemon juice and salt and rub evenly over the surface of the chicken.

2. Place the saffron threads in a small cup and pour the boiling water over them. Let the saffron mixture steep for 5 minutes, then pour it over the chicken. Allow the chicken to marinate in the refrigerator for at least 30 minutes.

3. To prepare the yogurt masala, combine the yogurt, garlic, ginger, cumin, cardamom, coriander, and cayenne and blend well.

4. Spread the yogurt masala evenly over the chicken, cover tightly, and marinate in the refrigerator for 12 to 24 hours.

5. Place the chicken on a rack in a roasting pan. Roast the chicken for 10 minutes in a 400°F, then reduce the heat to 325°F and roast it for an additional 15 minutes, or until it is fully cooked. Baste the chicken with hot clarified butter during roasting time.

PREPARATION NOTES

Instead of cutting up a whole roasting chicken, select whatever chicken pieces that you and your guests prefer. Remember to remove the skin if it hasn't already been removed.

Commercially prepared ground cumin, coriander, and cardamom seeds can also be used, although the masala's flavor is markedly better when the seeds are freshly toasted and ground.

The marinade will penetrate deeper where the chicken was scored, for extra flavor. Scoring also helps speed up the cooking.

SERVING SUGGESTIONS

Serve this spicy chicken dish with lime wedges, accompany with rice or another grain to help temper the heat of the cayenne pepper.

Nutritional information per serving: 280 calories; 33 grams protein; 14 grams fat; 4 grams carbohydrate; 165 milligrams sodium; 110 milligrams cholesterol.

Enchiladas Verdes

Enchiladas are filled and stuffed tortillas, topped with a sauce and baked. In this case, the sauce is prepared with tomatillos. They are related to the gooseberry and have papery husk that peels away easily. Look for tomatillos in the produce section of larger markets, or in smaller ethnic markets or *bodegas*.

Makes 12 enchiladas

2 teaspoons corn oil or *olive oil*
1 onion, cut into medium dice
1 garlic clove, finely minced
1 cup farmer's cheese or *pot cheese*
⅓ cup heavy cream
2 cups shredded, cooked chicken meat
3 tablespoons sliced almonds, toasted
½ teaspoon salt (or, to taste)
freshly ground black pepper to taste
2 cups quartered tomatillos
1 cup sliced scallions
⅔ cup chopped fresh cilantro
2 whole roasted jalapeños, seeded, and diced
2 tablespoons chopped fresh mint
½ teaspoon ground cumin seed
½ teaspoon ground coriander seed
12 corn tortillas
6 ounces Monterey Jack cheese, coarsely shredded

IN ADVANCE   Preheat the oven to 350°F. Lightly oil a baking dish (approximately 11 inches × 7 inches).

1.   Heat the oil in a small skillet over medium heat. Add the onion and garlic and sauté until the onion turns a light golden brown, about 6 to 8 minutes. Remove them from the heat, spread in a thin layer on a plate, and allow to cool completely.

2. Puree the farmer's cheese in a food processor until smooth. With the machine running, add the heavy cream in a stream. Pour the cheese mixture into a bowl. Fold in the chicken and almonds. Add salt and pepper to taste. Refrigerate this mixture until needed.

3. Place the tomatillos, scallions, cilantro, jalapeños, mint, cumin, and coriander in the food processor or blender and puree to form a sauce. Place the sauce in a shallow bowl. Add salt and pepper to taste.

4. Heat a cast-iron or other heavy-bottomed skillet over medium heat until quite hot. Soften the tortillas by toasting each one in the skillet, about 15 seconds on each side. Dip the heated tortillas into the sauce, one at a time, to coat very lightly. Set the sauced tortillas on a work surface. Place a tablespoon of the filling on the tortilla, slightly off-center, then roll it up into a cylinder.

5. Place the filled and rolled enchiladas in a buttered or oiled baking dish. Repeat this procedure with the remaining tortillas until all have been filled and rolled.

6. Spoon the remaining sauce over the enchiladas. Scatter the cheese over them, cover the pan, and bake in a 350°F oven for 15 minutes.

PREPARATION NOTES

Use leftover chicken from a roast, or poach a chicken breast or thighs in chicken stock or broth.

For a vegetarian rendition of this entrée, substitute a variety of vegetables for the cooked chicken. The vegetables should be steamed, then chopped or diced and added to the cheese mixture.

The recipe may be completed through step 3 up to one day in advance. For best results, however, toast and fill the tortillas just before baking them in the sauce.

SERVING SUGGESTIONS

Serve with a fresh tomato salsa, rice, and sour cream.

Nutritional information per enchilada: 160 calories; 9 grams protein; 7 grams fat; 17 grams carbohydrate; 105 milligrams sodium; 15 milligrams cholesterol.

Grilled Chicken with Fennel

To ensure that the chicken cooks quickly and evenly, lightly pound the breasts to an even thickness. Place each breast between two pieces of waxed paper and, using a wooden meat mallet or a small heavy skillet, work from the center of the breast outward, stretching the chicken with each stroke.

Makes 4 servings

2 tablespoons extra-virgin olive oil or peanut oil
1 tablespoon lime juice
2 cloves garlic, crushed
½ teaspoon fennel seeds, cracked
½ teaspoon salt
¼ teaspoon freshly ground black pepper
4 chicken breasts, boneless and skinless
1 tablespoon unsalted butter
2 teaspoons finely minced shallots
2 cups thinly sliced or shaved fennel
Pernod to taste (optional)

IN ADVANCE   Clean the rack of your grill. Preheat the grill or start the charcoal. The fire should be hot (glowing coals with a light cover of ash).

1.   Combine the olive oil, lime juice, garlic, fennel, salt, and pepper in a shallow baking dish.

2.   Blot the chicken dry with paper toweling and add it to the olive-oil-and-lime marinade. Turn to coat the chicken evenly and marinate for about 1 hour.

3. Remove the chicken from the marinade scraping off any excess by wiping the breasts against the edge of the baking dish. Place the chicken on the grill and cook without disturbing for 3 to 4 minutes. Then turn the breasts and continue to grill for another 4 to 5 minutes. If the exterior of the chicken is cooking too quickly, move it to a cooler portion of the grill or raise the rack away from the heat.

4. Heat the butter in a skillet over medium heat. Add the shallots and sauté for about 3 minutes, stirring frequently.

5. Add the fennel, stirring to coat it evenly with the butter and shallots. Season well with salt and pepper, then cover the skillet and allow the mixture to steam in its own juices for about 5 minutes, or until the fennel is quite limp. Add a few drops of Pernod if desired.

6. Serve the chicken on a nest of the fennel.

PREPARATION NOTES

To crush garlic cloves, place the broad side of your knife blade against the cloves, then pound the blade smartly with the side of your fist. This will not only crush the garlic, it will also loosen the papery skin, making it easier to slip off.

Instead of grilling the chicken, you could also bake it in the marinade. Preheat the oven to 375 or 400°F and bake the chicken, loosely covered, for about 15 minutes (longer if the chicken breast is more than ½-inch thick).

For an entirely different taste, replace the fennel with asparagus tips, celery, or diced cucumber (peeled and seeded).

SERVING SUGGESTIONS

Potato Puree with Roasted Eggplant and Garlic (page 224) or a Potato Gratin (page 226) would be appropriate with this dish, along with a selection of steamed or boiled seasonal vegetables.

Nutritional information per serving: 225 calories; 28 grams protein; 11 grams fat; 3 grams carbohydrate; 350 milligrams sodium; 75 milligrams cholesterol.

Herbed Breaded Chicken with Creamy Mustard Gravy

Makes 4 servings

1 teaspoon cornstarch
1 cup chicken stock
¼ cup evaporated skim milk
1 tablespoon Dijon-style mustard
1¼ pounds chicken breasts, boneless and skinless
¼ cup cornmeal
½ cup crushed corn flakes
1 teaspoon chopped fresh chives
1 teaspoon chopped fresh thyme leaves
1 teaspoon chopped fresh parsley
½ cup buttermilk

IN ADVANCE   This dish is an example of how a traditional favorite, in this case, fried chicken, can be prepared with less fat, yet still produce the rich flavor and crisp texture we expect. Corn flake crumbs replace the traditional breading, and the chicken is baked instead of fried. The classic "milk gravy" made in the pan with some of the cooking fat is replaced with a sauce that adds virtually no fat to the dish.

1.   Dissolve the cornstarch completely in a tablespoon of the stock. Bring the remaining stock a boil, then reduce the heat to medium and add the dissolved cornstarch. Continue to simmer until the stock is thickened.

2.   Add the milk and mustard to the thickened stock. Remove the sauce from the heat.

3.   Trim the chicken of any visible fat. Pat dry with absorbent toweling.

4.   Combine the cornmeal, corn flakes, and the herbs in a small bowl.

5. Place the buttermilk in another bowl. To bread the chicken, first dip it into the buttermilk, then into the cornmeal mixture, coating the pieces evenly. Place the breaded chicken in a baking dish. (For the best results, use a small rack if available.)

6. Bake the chicken in a 375°F oven for about 20 minutes, or until the juices run clear and the breading is golden brown and crisp.

7. Return the sauce to low heat and bring it to a simmer. Check the seasoning. If necessary, add mustard to taste. To serve, pool the sauce on heated plates or a platter and place the chicken on top of the sauce.

PREPARATION NOTES

Whole chicken legs, rabbit, turkey steaks, or lean white fish can each be used to replace the chicken breasts.

The sauce can be prepared several hours in advance, or even the day before. Reheat it gently and avoid boiling, as cornstarch can break down if it is overheated.

Use a grainy mustard to give this entrée's sauce a little extra texture. Also feel free to experiment with flavored mustards—for example, those containing herbs or peppercorns.

SERVING SUGGESTIONS

A bowl of fresh steamed peas and a basket of corn sticks or muffins are ideal side dishes.

Nutritional information per serving: 230 calories; 37 grams protein; 3 grams fat; 13 grams carbohydrate; 215 milligrams sodium; 85 milligrams cholesterol.

Poule-au-Pot

This a classic French dish, whose name translates as "chicken in the pot," is well-suited to meals served *en famille*, or family-style. The richly flavored broth is served as the first course, followed by a platter heaped with the chicken and vegetables. Its simple, honest flavors can hardly be improved upon.

Makes 4 servings

1 "fryer" chicken (about 3 pounds)
½ teaspoon salt
freshly ground pepper to taste
5 to 6 sprigs of fresh herbs (thyme, tarragon, and/or parsley)
2 quarts (8 cups) chicken broth, (or as needed)
1 leek, split lengthwise
1 whole garlic clove, peeled
1 celery stalk, sliced thin
1 carrot, sliced thin
12 pearl onions, peeled
1 parsnip, sliced thin
1 fennel stalk, sliced thin
1 cup cooked rice or noodles
1 cup green peas, fresh or frozen
2 tablespoons chopped fresh parsley

IN ADVANCE   Tie the leek, celery, garlic clove, and half of the herb stems together with twine to form a *bouquet garni*.

1.   Rinse the chicken in cool water, then pat dry. Lightly season the cavity of the bird with salt and pepper. Place half of the fresh herbs in the cavity.

2.   Place the chicken, breastside down, in a pot large enough to accommodate both the bird and the vegetables comfortably. Add the broth to the pot. (There should be enough to cover the bird by 2 inches.)

3. Place the pot over medium heat. Slowly bring the broth to just under a boil.

4. Add the *bouquet garni* of leek, celery, garlic clove, and herb stems to the simmering stock.

5. Reduce the heat to low and poach the chicken for about 20 to 30 minutes, skimming the surface as necessary to remove any foam or grease that rises to the surface. Add more stock as necessary to keep the bird completely submerged.

6. Add the carrot, pearl onions, celery, parsnip, and fennel to the pot. Continue to poach the bird until it is fully cooked and the vegetables are tender to the bite, for about another 15 to 20 minutes.

7. Remove the chicken from the broth and set it on a platter. Allow it to rest a few minutes, then slice the chicken.

8. Strain the broth. Place the sliced chicken and vegetables on a heated platter and ladle a few spoonfuls of the broth over them. Cover loosely and keep warm in a 200°F oven until ready to serve.

9. Return the strained broth to the pot and return it to a simmer. Add the rice or noodles, peas, and chopped parsley to the broth, and taste the broth. If necessary, adjust the seasonings with salt and pepper.

10. Serve the broth in cups, then follow it with the sliced chicken and vegetables as a second course.

PREPARATION NOTES

If available, a free-range chicken will give this dish an incomparable depth of flavor and body, as will a good-quality, homemade chicken broth.

Leeks can hold a surprising amount of dirt between their leaves. To clean, cut away the roots and tougher green ends. Halve or quarter the leek lengthwise—from white bulb to green end—and rinse thoroughly.

SERVING SUGGESTIONS

This meal's accompaniments are simple and few: a crusty loaf of a peasant-style bread, a salad, and, if you wish, a wedge of a *Brie* or *Camembert* served with fresh fruit served afterward.

Nutritional information per serving: 370 calories; 48 grams protein; 11 grams fat; 7 grams carbohydrate; 405 milligrams sodium; 120 milligrams cholesterol.

Ossobuco Milanese

Ossobuco translates roughly as "bone with a hole." In Milan, where this dish originates, the addition of a mixture of parsley, garlic, anchovy, and lemon zest, the *gremolada*, provides a piquant counterpoint to the richly-flavored tender veal shank.

Makes 4 servings

4 pieces veal shank (about 12 ounces each)
½ teaspoon salt
freshly ground pepper to taste
2 tablespoons vegetable oil
flour as needed for dredging
1 large yellow onion, diced
1 carrot, diced
1 leek, sliced
2 to 3 cloves garlic, minced fine
3 tablespoons tomato paste
¾ cup dry white wine
4 cups beef broth
1 to 2 teaspoons cornstarch (optional)
1 teaspoon finely grated lemon zest
3 tablespoons chopped fresh flat-leaf parsley
2 anchovy fillets, chopped

IN ADVANCE Preheat the oven to 325°F.

1. Season the veal shanks liberally with salt and pepper. Then dredge them in flour and shake away any excess.

2. Heat the oil in an ovenproof casserole or dutch oven over high heat. Sear the seasoned shanks in the oil, turning them until they take on a light golden brown color, about 2 to 3 minutes on each side. Transfer the shanks to a platter and cover loosely to keep them warm.

3. Drain off all but about 1 tablespoon of oil from the pan. Add the onion, carrot, leek, and half of the garlic to the hot oil and sauté over medium heat, stirring frequently, for about 10 minutes, or until the onion turns a deep golden brown.

4. Add the tomato paste and stir well. Sauté for an additional 2 to 3 minutes, stirring frequently, until the tomato paste turns a rust color.

5. Add the wine and stir well to dissolve the tomato paste. Add the broth, then bring the liquid up to a bare simmer. Return the veal shanks to the pan and check the level of the liquid: there should be enough to cover the shanks by three-quarters. Cover the pan and place it in the preheated oven.

6. Braise the shanks in the oven for 1½ to 2 hours. Test for doneness by lifting the largest shank with a kitchen fork. The shank should slide easily off the fork, if it is properly cooked. Transfer the shanks to a serving platter and keep warm while finishing the sauce.

7. Strain the braising liquid, then return it to the casserole and bring it to a full boil over high heat. Skim away any fat that rises to the surface. Lower the heat to medium, and continue to simmer the sauce until it begins to thicken. To save time, add a little cornstarch diluted in broth or water to thicken the sauce.

8. After it is properly thickened, taste the sauce and add salt and pepper if needed.

9. Combine the remaining garlic, the lemon zest, parsley and anchovy fillets to form the gremolada.

10. To serve, ladle the sauce over the shanks, and scatter with the gremolada.

PREPARATION NOTES

The veal shank for this dish should be cut from the hind leg, which is meatier than the foreleg shank. Ask the butcher to cut the shank into 1½- to 2-inch-thick pieces and tie them around the middle.

This recipe may be prepared through step 5, then refrigerated overnight before completing the remaining steps. Preparing the shanks the day before will give the flavors a chance to mellow. This will also harden the fat that rises to the surface of the sauce, making it easy to remove.

SERVING SUGGESTIONS

For a traditional presentation, serve the shanks with a risotto and a medley of brightly colored steamed or boiled vegetables (see Risotto with Asparagus Tips, page 180).

Nutritional information per serving: 355 calories; 33 grams protein; 19 grams fat; 12 grams carbohydrate; 360 milligrams sodium; 135 milligrams cholesterol.

Swiss-style Shredded Veal

The combination of lightly sautéed veal strips and a suave, creamy sauce makes this dish a guaranteed success. This delicious recipe has likely evolved from the thrifty use of meat usually remaining from the loin after medallions or cutlets of veal are cut.

Makes 4 servings

IN ADVANCE Reduce 1½ cups of rich, homemade stock or broth to ½ cup by rapidly boiling over medium heat.

1¼ pounds veal cutlets (cut from the leg)
⅔ cup all-purpose flour
½ teaspoon salt
¼ teaspoon freshly ground black pepper
1 tablespoon vegetable oil
1 tablespoon finely minced shallots
¼ pound mushrooms, trimmed and sliced thin
½ cup dry white wine
½ cup reduced chicken stock
¼ cup heavy cream
1 tablespoon brandy
freshly squeezed lemon juice to taste

1. Cut the veal into thin strips and pat them dry with absorbent toweling.

2. Combine the flour with salt and pepper in a shallow bowl. Add the veal strips and coat them well with the seasoned flour. Transfer the veal to a sieve or colander and shake to remove any excess flour. (Discard any leftover flour.)

3. Heat the oil in a large skillet over medium-high heat. When the oil is very hot, add the veal and sauté, stirring from time to time, for about 10 minutes, or until it is browned. Remove the veal with a slotted spoon to a heated platter, cover loosely, and keep warm while completing the sauce.

4. Pour off all but a thin film of oil from the skillet, and return it to medium heat. Allow the pan to get quite hot. Add the shallots and mushrooms to the pan, and sauté (again, stirring only once in a while) until any moisture released from the mushrooms has cooked away.

5. Add the wine, reduced stock, heavy cream, and brandy to the pan. Simmer the sauce for about 3 to 4 minutes, then return the veal to the pan. Stir until the veal is evenly coated and heated. Serve the veal with the sauce.

PREPARATION NOTES

This dish is prepared by sautéing, so it is crucial that the meat not "stew" in its own juices as it cooks. Be sure that you allow enough time for the pan and the oil to heat up. Then add the meat in a single layer to the pan, and let it cook without stirring for at least 2 or 3 minutes; after that, stir only occasionally.

Use skinless and boneless chicken or turkey to replace the veal if desired. If wild mushrooms are not available, use domestic mushrooms, or try reconstituting dried mushrooms and adding them to the dish. To cut back on calories, substitute a $^{50}/_{50}$ mixture of sour cream and plain low-fat yogurt for the heavy cream.

SERVING SUGGESTIONS

Roësti Potatoes, a sautéed cake of grated potatoes (see page 230), is traditionally served with this dish. Oven-roasted Potatoes (see page 240), broad egg noodles, or herb-flavored spatzli would go well.

Nutritional information per serving: 285 calories; 25 grams protein; 15 grams fat; 9 grams carbohydrate; 335 milligrams sodium; 130 milligrams cholesterol.

Sautéed Veal with Lump Crabmeat and Asparagus

When you see a sautéed veal dish listed on the menu of a fine restaurant, it is likely that the meat is a medallion cut from the loin. Such a cut is not easy to find, even in butcher shops. If you are planning a very special meal, though, it is worth searching out. The cutlets recommended for this version should come from the leg, and should be cut across the grain for the tenderest results.

Makes 4 servings

1½ cups chicken broth
½ cup dry white wine
2 tablespoons tarragon vinegar
1 teaspoon chopped fresh tarragon leaves
2 teaspoons minced shallots
a few drops of Worcestershire sauce
2 to 3 whole black peppercorns, cracked
1 bay leaf
⅓ cup evaporated skim milk
1 teaspoon cornstarch
¼ cup heavy cream
½ cup flour, or as needed
½ teaspoon salt
¼ teaspoon freshly ground pepper
4 veal cutlets, cut from the leg
1 tablespoon vegetable oil
6 ounces lump crabmeat, picked to remove shell or cartilage
12 asparagus spears, trimmed

IN ADVANCE   Steam or blanch the asparagus, then rinse in cool water. Drain them, and hold in the refrigerator.

1. Combine ¼ cup of the broth, the wine, vinegar, tarragon, shallots, Worcestershire sauce, peppercorns, and bay leaf in a small saucepan. Bring the mixture to a boil and let it reduce to a syrupy consistency.

2. Add the remaining chicken broth, the milk and the heavy cream, then return the liquid to a full boil.

3. Dilute the cornstarch in a teaspoon of cold water and add it to the simmering sauce. Return to a boil once again, then reduce the heat. Simmer for 2 minutes, then check the seasoning. Add additional vinegar, chopped tarragon, or freshly ground pepper to taste if needed. Set aside.

4. Combine the flour, salt, and pepper in a shallow dish.

5. Trim any visible fat from the cutlets, and pat them dry with absorbent toweling. Dredge the cutlets in the seasoned flour and shake off any excess.

6. Heat the oil in a skillet over high heat. Add the veal, working in batches if necessary to avoid overcrowding the pan. Sauté on the first side for about 2 minutes, then reduce the heat to medium and turn the cutlets, sauté for another 3 minutes. Transfer the veal to a baking dish, cover loosely, and keep warm while sautéing any remaining veal.

7. Return the sauce to the stovetop and heat to a simmer. Add about 2 tablespoons of the heated sauce to the crabmeat to warm it. Pool the remaining sauce on heated plates or a serving platter, arrange cutlets on the plates, and top with the warmed crabmeat. Arrange the asparagus around the veal and serve at once.

PREPARATION NOTES

If you prefer, you can also prepare this dish with turkey or chicken breast cut into scallops and lightly pounded.

The sauce can be prepared through step 3, then cooled and refrigerated for up to 2 days. When reheating the sauce, heat it to just under a boil, then immediately lower the heat to prevent the cornstarch from breaking down.

A rice pilaf flavored with leeks and a medley of fresh spring vegetables that have been lightly stewed in vegetable stock, flavored with fresh herbs, and finished with a bit of fresh sweet butter would make this a wonderful meal.

Nutritional information per serving: 330 calories; 33 grams protein; 17 grams fat; 9 grams carbohydrate; 460 milligrams sodium; 160 milligrams cholesterol.

Stewed Rabbit with Prunes

While for many people rabbit remains an unfamiliar food, farm-raised rabbit is more widely available than ever before. Rabbit, like other game meats, is lower in fat and cholesterol than domestic meats. It can be found in the meat cases of most large supermarkets, or by special order from butchers.

Rabbit has a rich, "gamey" flavor that marries well with the other ingredients in this savory stew. Feel free, however, to replace the rabbit with chicken pieces, which will reduce the cooking time to about 35 minutes.

Makes 4 servings

1 rabbit, cut into pieces
½ cup all-purpose flour
1 teaspoon salt
½ teaspoon ground black pepper
1 tablespoon corn oil
1 tablespoon minced shallots
1 carrot, sliced thin
1 stalk celery, sliced thin
1 yellow onion, sliced thin
½ cup dry white wine
4 to 5 cups chicken broth
1 sprig fresh thyme (or ½ teaspoon dried leaves)
1 bay leaf
⅓ cup whole pitted prunes
2 tablespoons red currant jelly
1 tablespoon cornstarch (optional)
1 to 2 teaspoons Dijon-style mustard (or to taste)
unsweetened prune juice to taste

IN ADVANCE Preheat the oven to 325°F.

1. Trim any visible fat from the rabbit pieces, and then pat them dry with absorbent toweling.

2. Combine the flour, salt, and pepper in a shallow dish. Dredge the rabbit in the seasoned flour and shake off any excess.

3. Heat the oil in a large skillet over high heat. Add the rabbit pieces to the oil and sear on all sides to golden brown. Transfer the rabbit pieces to a platter.

4. Pour off all but enough oil to lightly coat the skillet. Add the shallots, carrot, celery, and onion to the and sauté over medium heat, stirring from time to time, until the onion turns golden brown, about 8 to 10 minutes.

5. Add the wine to the skillet and stir well to release any drippings. Allow the wine to cook away almost completely.

6. Return the rabbit to the skillet and add enough broth to barely cover the pieces. Bring the broth to a simmer, add the thyme and bay leaf, and then cover.

7. Braise the rabbit over low heat, or in a 325°F oven, for about 1 hour or until very tender. Transfer the rabbit to a platter, cover loosely, and keep warm while finishing the sauce.

8. Raise the heat to high and bring the sauce to a boil. Reduce the heat slightly and skim away any fat from the surface. Add the prunes and red currant jelly. Simmer until all the ingredients are blended and heated through.

9. Dilute the cornstarch with a little white wine, stock, or water and add it to the simmering sauce to thicken it slightly. (This step may not be necessary if the sauce has thickened slightly while cooking.) Taste the sauce and adjust the seasonings as needed by adding a little prepared mustard, prune juice, salt, or freshly ground pepper.

10. Return the rabbit pieces to the skillet, along with any juices that may have accumulated on the platter. Turn the pieces to reheat them and to coat evenly with the sauce. Serve the rabbit on heated plates or a serving platter with the sauce and prunes.

This dish can be prepared through step 7, then refrigerated for up to 2 days or frozen for up to a month. The sauce should be completed just before serving. If you are freezing this dish to serve later, date and label it, indicating what needs to be done to finish it.

Accompaniments of barley or bulgur pilaf or broad egg noodles, paired with brussels sprouts or braised red cabbage, would complement this meal well.

Nutritional information per serving: 380 calories; 35 grams protein; 16 grams fat; 22 grams carbohydrate; 610 milligrams sodium; 95 milligrams cholesterol.

Beef Goulash

Goulash is a hearty stew that can be simmered on top of the stove, or cooked slowly in a moderate oven. The primary advantage to cooking braises and stews such as this one in the stove is that the finished dish rarely scorches or overcooks into shreds.

Makes 8 servings

2 tablespoons vegetable oil
1 large yellow onion, chopped
1 tablespoon vinegar (or to taste)
3 tablespoons mild Hungarian paprika
¾ teaspoon dried marjoram leaves
3 cloves garlic, minced fine
1 teaspoon lemon zest
1 teaspoon salt (or to taste)
⅓ cup tomato paste
6 to 7 cups beef broth
3½ pounds beef shank, cut into large cubes
freshly ground black pepper to taste

IN ADVANCE   If you will be cooking the goulash in the oven rather than on the stovetop, preheat the oven to 325°F.

1.   Heat the oil in a deep skillet over medium heat. Add the onions and sauté, stirring from time to time, until they are golden brown, about 8 to 10 minutes.

2.   Add the vinegar, paprika, marjoram, garlic, lemon zest, and salt to the onions and stir to distribute all of the ingredients evenly. Continue to sauté for another 2 minutes.

3.   Add the tomato paste and stir well. Sauté for about 3 minutes, stirring frequently, until the tomato paste turns a rust color.

4. Add the broth and stir thoroughly to dissolve the tomato paste. Bring the mixture to a boil.

5. Add the cubed beef, then check the level of the liquid: There should be just enough to cover the beef. If necessary, add a little broth or water. Lower the heat, then cover the pan and simmer gently on the stovetop or cook in a 325°F oven for about 1½ hours. The goulash is ready when the meat is extremely tender to the bite.

6. Remove the pan from the heat or oven, and skim away any grease that may have risen to the surface during cooking. Taste the sauce and add salt, pepper, or vinegar if necessary to adjust the seasoning.

PREPARATION NOTES

This dish's flavor improves when made a day in advance, and will freeze well. You can use canned beef broth, but look for a low-sodium brand. Beef bouillon cubes, however, are too salty for this dish.

SERVING SUGGESTIONS

Beef goulash's classic accompaniments include spaetzli (traditional German-style dumplings made from a pourable batter), broad egg noodles, or bread dumplings. A bowlful of steamed baby peas served with a knob of sweet butter is another excellent choice.

Nutritional information per serving: 270 calories; 36 grams protein; 12 grams fat; 7 grams carbohydrate; 350 milligrams sodium; 75 milligrams cholesterol.

Poached Tenderloin with
Green Peppercorn Sabayon

The sabayon sauce (*zabaglione* in Italian) in this recipe is a savory version of the sweet dessert sauce made from egg yolks, *marsala*, and sugar. The egg yolks are beaten with a little of the liquid used to poach the beef. Cooking and whipping the yolks along with the green peppercorns creates a thick foamy sauce that has a light texture and flavor.

Makes 4 servings

1¼-pound beef tenderloin
5 cups beef broth or *consommé*
1 leek, trimmed and sliced thinly on the bias
1 carrot, sliced thinly
1 celery stalk, sliced thinly
1 egg yolk
1 tablespoon green peppercorns, drained and mashed
½ teaspoon salt
freshly squeezed lemon juice to taste

IN ADVANCE   Trim the tenderloin of any surface fat. Pat it dry, and season the beef well with salt and pepper. Wrap butcher's twine around the tenderloin and tighten slightly, then tie a knot. Cut the string, and repeat the process at 2-inch intervals the entire length of the tenderloin.

1.   Combine the broth, leek, carrot, and celery in a deep skillet large enough to accommodate the beef. Bring the broth to a boil over high heat, then lower the heat to a bare simmer.

2.   Add the tenderloin and poach it until it is cooked to the desired doneness. (For medium rare, cook to an internal temperature of 135 to 140°F, about 20 to 25 minutes.)

3.   Remove the tenderloin from the poaching liquid and place it on a heated platter. Remove the twine, then cover the beef loosely and allow it to rest about 10 minutes before slicing it.

4. Combine ½ cup of the poaching liquid, the egg yolk, and the peppercorns in a stainless-steel bowl and whip well. Place the bowl over a saucepan of simmering water and continue to whip the sauce until it becomes thick and foamy, for about 5 to 6 minutes. Taste the sauce and add salt or a few drops of lemon juice if necessary to adjust the seasoning.

5. Ladle the sauce over the sliced tenderloin and serve at once.

PREPARATION NOTES

Tying the tenderloin will help give the meat a compact, uniform shape that allows it to cook evenly, and will also give the finished dish a more pleasant appearance. If you are unsure about how to tie a roast, ask the butcher to do it for you.

SERVING SUGGESTIONS

A selection of grilled or roasted vegetables (zucchini, eggplant, tomatoes, and/or bell peppers) would be a good accompaniment to this dish.

Nutritional information per serving: 300 calories; 37 grams protein; 14 grams fat; 6 grams carbohydrate; 460 milligrams sodium; 170 milligrams cholesterol.

Carbonnades of Beef Flamande

Carbonnades is French for "meat cooked over coals." This savory combination of beef and onions cooked in a dark, rich ale is a classic example from the Belgians of how to make the most from the ingredients at hand. Stout or porter would also work well in this hearty braised dish.

Makes 4 servings

4 beef chuck steaks (about 5 to 6 ounces each)
½ teaspoon salt
freshly ground black pepper to taste
3 to 4 tablespoons vegetable oil
4 onions, thickly sliced
¼ cup tomato paste
¼ cup water
2 tablespoons dark brown sugar, tightly packed
1 bottle (12 ounces) dark beer
2 cups beef broth
1 tablespoon Dijon-style mustard
2 teaspoons balsamic vinegar

1. Season the steaks generously with salt and pepper.

2. Heat the vegetable oil in a cast-iron skillet over high heat. Add the steaks and sear them on both sides, about 2 minutes per side. Remove the steaks from the skillet and set aside on a plate.

3. Add the onions to the skillet and sauté them until they turn a deep golden brown, about 8 to 10 minutes. Stir them from time to time as they cook to prevent scorching.

4. Add the tomato paste to the onions, and sauté for about 3 minutes over medium heat, stirring frequently. Add the water and brown sugar and stir well.

5. Add the beer and stir to blend. Allow the cooking liquid to reduce to half its original volume. Add the broth, then lower the heat to a simmer.

6. Return the steaks to the skillet, along with any juices that have accumulated on the plate. Cover the skillet and place in a 300°F oven. Braise the steaks until they are very tender, for about 1½ hours.

7. Remove the steaks from the skillet and keep them warm. Bring the sauce to a simmer over medium heat. Skim any fat from the surface, then add the mustard and balsamic vinegar. Allow the sauce to reduce slightly over high heat, and check seasoning. Add more salt, pepper, mustard, or vinegar if needed.

8. Ladle the sauce over the steaks and serve.

PREPARATION NOTES

This recipe can be prepared in advance through step 6, then refrigerated for a day or two; the flavor will often improve with a little time to "mellow." Reheat gently in a 325°F oven or over low heat on the stovetop.

Choose cuts from the shoulder or the bottom round, as they are the most flavorful and stand up best to this long, slow-cooking technique.

SERVING SUGGESTIONS

Broad noodles, steamed potatoes, or potato croquettes would all make excellent accompaniments to this rich, savory beef dish.

Nutritional information per serving: 520 calories; 43 grams protein; 24 grams fat; 22 grams carbohydrate; 810 milligrams sodium; 140 milligrams cholesterol.

Grilled Flank Steak with Pineapple and Roasted Shallots

The key to grilling flank steaks (or any other food) is a thoroughly preheated grill. Scrub the grill before starting to remove any debris that might cause the steak to stick.

Makes 6 servings

1 flank steak (about 1½ pounds)
1 cup unsweetened pineapple juice
1 cup crushed fresh pineapple
½ cup sliced red onion
1 tablespoon reduced-sodium soy sauce
1 tablespoon red-wine vinegar
2 tablespoons olive oil
1 lime, thinly sliced
3 tablespoons chopped fresh cilantro leaves
2 cloves garlic, minced fine
2 teaspoons minced jalapeño, or to taste
1 tablespoon mild chili powder
a few drops Tabasco sauce
½ cup beef broth
6 to 8 whole shallots, roasted and shredded

IN ADVANCE   Be sure that the grill is properly preheated and that the rack has been cleaned.

1.   Trim any visible fat from the flank steak and place it in a shallow dish. Add all of the remaining ingredients, except for the broth and roasted shallots.

2.   Turn the steak a few times to coat it evenly, then let it to marinate for at least 2 hours, or overnight in the refrigerator.

3. When ready to grill, lightly rub the rods of the rack with a little vegetable oil and remove any excess with a clean cloth.

4. Remove the steak from the marinade and scrape off any excess. Grill the steak on one side for about 6 to 7 minutes, then turn the steak and cook to the desired doneness.

5. While the steak is grilling, transfer the marinade to a saucepan and bring it to a full boil. Add the broth and continue to simmer for another 5 minutes. Taste the sauce and add lime juice, Tabasco sauce, or cilantro to taste if needed.

6. Allow the steak to rest for about 10 minutes, then slice it thinly on an angle. Serve the steak topped with the sauce and sprinkle with the shallots.

PREPARATION NOTES

Skirt or sirloin steaks would also be suitable for this recipe. Try using the marinade for chicken pieces or pork chops.

SERVING SUGGESTIONS

A corn or pepper relish, steamed asparagus or green beans, and grilled sweet potatoes or yams would make excellent accompaniments to this dish.

Nutritional information per serving: 200 calories; 23 grams protein; 7 grams fat; 13 grams carbohydrate; 165 milligrams sodium; 60 milligrams cholesterol.

Beef Tenderloin with
Blue Cheese and Herb Crust

This recipe, one of the most popular menu offerings at St. Andrew's Cafe.

Makes 4 servings

4 steaks cut from the beef tenderloin (about 4 ounces each)
1 slice white bread, toasted
2 tablespoons crumbed blue cheese
2 tablespoons chopped fresh parsley
2 tablespoons chopped fresh chives
¼ teaspoon freshly ground white pepper

IN ADVANCE   Preheat the oven to 375°F.

1.   Trim any remaining visible fat from the beef, and pat it dry with absorbent toweling. Refrigerate the steaks while preparing the crust.

2.   Combine the bread, blue cheese, parsley, chives, and pepper in a food processor. Run the machine until the mixture reaches an even texture.

3.   Heat a nonstick or cast-iron skillet over medium-high heat. When the pan is quite hot, add the steaks. Allow them to cook on one side without disturbing them for about 2 to 3 minutes. Turn them once, and sear them for another 2 to 3 minutes on the second side.

4.   Remove the steaks from the skillet and place them on a rack set in a baking dish. Pat the blue cheese and herb mixture evenly over the steaks, then bake them in the oven for 15 minutes, or until they reach the desired doneness.

The meat should be cut into medallions, which are prepared by cutting even slices from a section of tenderloin. It is easy to do yourself with a sharp knife, but your butcher can do it for you, or you can purchase them already cut.

Use any lean, tender cut of beef in this recipe. For an even lower-fat version, substitute chicken breast or turkey steaks.

SERVING SUGGESTIONS

Potato Gratin (see page 226) makes a delicious side dish for this entrée. Select a fresh vegetable and serve it simply steamed or tossed with a light vinaigrette to complete the plate.

Nutritional information per serving: 240 calories; 30 grams protein; 12 grams fat; 4 grams carbohydrate; 200 milligrams sodium; 85 milligrams cholesterol.

Roast Loin of Pork with a Honey-Mustard Glaze

Pork that has been properly roasted is moist and delicious, even as leftovers. If you would like to have enough roast pork to make a wonderful salad or sandwich, double all of the ingredients. The cooking time will remain about the same for the roast, even when doubled.

Makes 6 servings

2 pounds boneless pork loin, trimmed and tied
1½ cups chicken broth
1 clove garlic, finely minced
1 tablespoon finely minced shallots
2 teaspoons fresh thyme leaves
1 tablespoon tomato paste
1 tablespoon Pommerey mustard
½ teaspoon cracked black peppercorns
4 teaspoons honey
1 tablespoon red wine vinegar

IN ADVANCE   Preheat the oven to 375°F.

1.   Remove any visible fat from the pork loin, and pat it dry with absorbent toweling.

2.   Heat a cast-iron or nonstick skillet over high heat. Add the pork loin and sear it on all sides (including the ends) until the meat takes on a light golden color. Remove the pork to a rack set in a baking or roasting pan.

3.   Reduce the heat to medium, add about 2 tablespoons of the broth to the pan, and stir well to dissolve any drippings. Add the garlic, shallots, and thyme leaves, and allow them to "stew" lightly in the broth.

4. Add the tomato paste to the pan, and sauté, stirring frequently, for about 2 minutes over low heat. Add the mustard, peppercorns, honey, and vinegar, and raise the heat to bring the mixture to a boil.

5. Return the pork to the pan and turn it to coat evenly with the glaze. Place the pork back on the rack and place it in the preheated oven.

6. Roast the pork to an internal temperature of 150°F (about 20 to 25 minutes, depending upon the diameter of the roast).

7. Remove the pork from the oven and set it on a heated platter, loosely covered to keep it warm. Let the pork rest for 15 minutes while you complete the sauce.

8. Add the remaining broth to the baking dish to dissolve any drippings (as long as they are not scorched). Add them to the skillet containing the unused portion of the glaze, along with the unused portion of the stock. Raise the heat to medium and let the sauce simmer for 5 to 6 minutes. Taste the sauce and add thyme leaves, red wine vinegar, or mustard to taste if needed.

9. Remove the twine from the pork, slice it evenly, and place the slices on heated plates or a platter. Pour or ladle the sauce over the sliced pork.

PREPARATION NOTES

This glaze can be prepared separately, then used to coat chops or chicken pieces before they are grilled. It is also perfect as a glaze for roast duck.

SERVING SUGGESTIONS

Spicy black beans flavored with chili and peppers and a dash of vinegar, Quinoa Pilaf with Red and Yellow Peppers (see page 174), or zucchini sautéed with fresh tomatoes and basil are all good side dishes.

Nutritional information per serving: 315 calories; 32 grams protein; 18 grams fat; 5 grams carbohydrate; 145 milligrams sodium; 130 milligrams cholesterol.

Pork Tenderloin with Apples and Caraway

Granny Smith apples are tart and hold their shape during cooking. If you are not certain which pesticides were used on the apples, you should peel them. Organically grown apples, which are cultivated without chemical pesticides and are available in many supermarkets, can be used without being peeled.

Makes 4 servings

1¼-pound pork tenderloin, trimmed
½ teaspoon caraway seeds
½ teaspoon salt
¼ teaspoon pepper
1 tablespoon vegetable oil
¼ cup applejack or apple-flavored brandy
½ cup chicken broth
2 tablespoons unsalted butter
1 Granny Smith apple, cored and thinly sliced

IN ADVANCE   Preheat the oven to 350°F.

1.   Pat the pork dry with absorbent toweling. Rub the caraway seeds, salt, and pepper evenly over the surface.

2.   Heat the vegetable oil in a cast-iron skillet over medium-high heat. Sear the tenderloin evenly on all sides (about 7 to 8 minutes total). Transfer it to a baking dish and place it in the preheated oven. Reserve the drippings in the skillet to use in the sauce.

3.   Roast the tenderloin, uncovered, for about 20 minutes, or until it has reached an internal temperature of 150°F. Remove the pork from the oven, place it on a heated platter, cover it loosely, and allow it to rest while you prepare the sauce.

4. Add half of the broth to the baking dish to dissolve the drippings in the bottom. These will be added to the sauce.

5. Pour off the oil from the skillet used to sear the pork, then place it over medium heat. Add the applejack and scrape the pan well to dissolve the drippings. Add the drippings from the baking dish and the remaining broth to the skillet and bring the sauce to a simmer.

6. Continue to simmer the sauce until it is slightly reduced and has a deep flavor, about 5 minutes. While the sauce is cooking, slice the pork and arrange it on a platter or on individual plates. Add any juices that may have accumulated on the platter to the sauce as well. Taste the sauce and add a little salt and pepper if necessary.

7. Remove the sauce from the heat and use a whisk or a fork to swirl the butter into the sauce. As soon as it is completely blended, pour or ladle the sauce over the sliced pork. Serve at once.

PREPARATION NOTES

The butter called for in step 7 can be omitted if desired.

SERVING SUGGESTIONS

Sweet Potato Cakes (see page 238), green beans with shallots, and glazed carrots are a few options for completing this entrée.

Nutritional information per serving: 380 calories; 29 grams protein; 25 grams fat; 8 grams carbohydrate; 370 milligrams sodium; 135 milligrams cholesterol.

Pork with Apricots, Currants, and Pine Nuts

Combining dried fruits with pork is a time-honored idea. The sweet-tart flavors of the dried fruit act as a perfect foil to the rich, succulent flavor of the pork.

Makes 4 servings

¼ cup dried currants
¼ cup diced dried apricots
4 pork chops, cut from the rib or loin (about 6 ounces each)
2 tablespoons vegetable oil
flour as needed
1 cup chicken broth
3 tablespoons brandy
2 tablespoons pine nuts, toasted

IN ADVANCE   Preheat the oven to 325°F. Place the currants and apricots in a small bowl. Add enough warm water to cover, and allow them to soak while preparing the pork chops.

1.   Trim away any visible fat from the pork chops and pat dry with absorbent toweling. Rub with a little salt and pepper to season.

2.   Heat the oil in a skillet over high heat. Dredge the chops in the flour and shake off any excess. Place the chops in the hot oil and sauté on one side for about 3 minutes, or until they take on a rich brown color. Turn them and sauté for an additional 2 or 3 minutes.

3.   Remove the chops from the skillet and place them in a baking dish. Bake them, uncovered, for about 10 to 12 minutes, or until the juices from the meat run clear. Remove the chops from the oven, place them on a heated platter, cover them loosely, and allow them to rest while preparing the sauce.

4. Add half of the broth to the baking dish to dissolve the drippings in the bottom. These will be added to the sauce.

5. Pour off the oil from the skillet used to sear the pork and place it over medium heat. Add the brandy and scrape the pan well to release the drippings. Add the drippings from the baking dish, and the remaining broth and bring the sauce to a simmer.

6. Simmer the sauce over medium heat for about 5 minutes, or until it is slightly reduced and the sauce develops a deep flavor. Add the plumped currants and apricots. Return the chops and any juices that may have accumulated on the platter to the skillet. Turn the chops to lightly coat them with the sauce. Taste the sauce and add a little salt and pepper, fresh herbs, and orange or lemon juice if desired.

7. Place the chops on heated plates or a serving platter, and ladle the sauce over them. Sprinkle with the toasted pine nuts. Serve at once.

PREPARATION NOTES

Reduce the cooking time by using pork cutlets instead of chops. Chicken breasts or turkey steaks would also work well. Toast the pine nuts in the oven, or sauté them in a dry skillet over medium heat. Keep a close eye on them as they brown, since they tend to burn quickly once they get hot. Experiment with other dried fruits, such as cherries, cranberries, blueberries, or prunes. Instead of plain water, consider using warmed red wine, port, or madeira to plump the dried fruit.

SERVING SUGGESTIONS

Prepare a selection of fresh seasonal vegetables by steaming or boiling them lightly. Toss them with fresh herbs and a splash of balsamic vinegar or fresh sweet cream.

Nutritional information per serving: 330 calories; 26 grams protein; 18 grams fat; 17 grams carbohydrate; 60 milligrams sodium; 70 milligrams cholesterol.

Lamb Chops with Artichokes

This recipe was created to showcase tiny tender artichokes. In Italy, where this dish originated, the arrival of the baby artichokes in the market is an event as eagerly awaited as the arrival of the first slender spears of asparagus in our country. Lamb, another traditional herald of spring, is a natural partner for the artichokes.

Makes 4 servings

4 whole artichokes
juice of 1 lemon
8 lamb chops (cut from the rib or loin)
4 tablespoons olive oil
1 tablespoon soy sauce
2 teaspoons fresh thyme leaves (or 1 teaspoon dried)
1 tablespoon minced shallots
1 clove garlic, finely minced
1 medium zucchini, cut into thick julienne
1 plum tomato, peeled, seeded, and chopped
1 tablespoon chopped pepperoncini

IN ADVANCE   Preheat the grill or broiler. Trim the leaves of the artichoke to remove the sharp ends, and use a spoon to scoop out the fuzzy "choke." Rub lemon on the cut edges of the artichoke to prevent it from discoloring.

1.   Place the artichokes in a shallow pan and add enough water to cover. Sprinkle with a tablespoon of the lemon juice and cover the pan. Simmer the artichokes gently for about 12 minutes, or until the bottoms can be easily pierced with the tip of a paring knife. Remove the artichokes from the cooking liquid and allow them to cool.

2.   When the artichokes are cool enough to handle easily, pull way the leaves and reserve them for garnish. Cut the bottoms into slices and set aside.

3. Trim the visible fat from the lamb chops, pat them dry with absorbent toweling, and place them in a shallow dish. Add half of the olive oil, the remaining lemon juice, soy sauce, thyme leaves, and salt and pepper to taste. Allow the chops to marinate for 2 to 3 hours in the refrigerator. Turn them once halfway through marination.

4. Heat the remaining olive oil in a sauté pan and add the shallots and garlic. Sauté, stirring frequently, for about 2 minutes. Add the zucchini and continue to sauté for another 3 minutes, then add the tomato and the sliced artichoke bottoms. Sauté for 4 minutes and add the pepperoncini. Taste the artichoke mixture and season to taste with additional salt, freshly ground pepper, and lemon juice if needed. Keep the mixture warm.

5. Grill or broil the lamb chops for about 4 minutes on each side, or to the desired doneness. Serve the lamb chops topped with the artichoke mixture.

PREPARATION NOTES

If you can find baby artichokes, they can be cooked and eaten whole, since the fuzzy "choke" hasn't developed yet. If baby artichokes are not available or out of season, fresh artichoke bottoms also yield excellent results. Failing that, frozen or canned artichoke hearts or bottoms would also do. If you use canned artichokes, be sure to select those which have been packed in brine rather than marinated.

This dish can be baked in the oven for a one-pan meal as follows: Marinate the chops as directed, and then quickly sear them in a cast-iron skillet. Transfer them to a platter, then prepare the artichoke mixture in the same pan (see step 4). Spread the mixture into an even layer, top with the lamb chops, and pour any remaining marinade over the chops. Cover loosely and bake in a 350°F oven for about 12 minutes, or until the chops are properly cooked.

SERVING SUGGESTIONS

Serve the lamb chops with pureed potatoes, a long-grain and wild-rice pilaf, or pan-fried or grilled polenta.

Nutritional information per serving: 380 calories; 42 grams protein; 15 grams fat; 17 grams carbohydrate; 445 milligrams sodium; 120 milligrams cholesterol.

Braised Lamb Shanks

Lamb shanks have a great deal of flavor, but because they come from the most exercised area of the animal it is important to allow them plenty of gentle cooking time to reach the buttery smooth, melt-in-your-mouth texture that is the hallmark of properly braised and stewed foods.

Makes 4 servings

4 lamb shanks
½ teaspoon salt
freshly ground black pepper to taste
all-purpose flour, as needed
1 tablespoon vegetable oil
2 garlic cloves, finely minced
1 yellow onion, diced
1 stalk celery, diced
1 carrot, diced
2 tablespoons tomato paste
¾ cup dry white wine
5 cups chicken broth
1 bay leaf
3 to 4 parsley stems

IN ADVANCE Preheat the oven to 325°F.

1. Remove any visible fat from the lamb shanks, pat them dry with absorbent toweling, and season them well with salt and pepper. Dredge them in flour and shake off any excess.

2. Heat the oil in a large skillet or flameproof casserole over high heat. Sear the lamb shanks on all sides until well-browned. Transfer them to a platter and cover loosely with foil to keep them warm.

3. Add the garlic, onion, celery, and carrot to the skillet and cook, stirring from time to time, until the onions are browned, about 7 to 8 minutes.

4. Add the tomato paste and stir to coat the vegetables evenly. Sauté for another 3 minutes.

5. Add the white wine and stir well. Continue to cook over high heat until the wine is reduced by about half. Add the broth, bay leaf, and parsley stems and bring the broth to a simmer.

6. Return the lamb shanks to the skillet and cover it tightly. Place the skillet in the preheated oven and let the shanks braise for about 1½ to 2 hours, or until the meat is easily pierced with a kitchen fork, or slides easily off the fork when lifted.

7. Remove the lamb shanks to a heated platter or warmed plates.

8. Strain the sauce, skim any fat from the surface, and bring it to a boil over medium heat. Taste it and adjust the seasonings with salt and pepper if needed. Pour or ladle the sauce over the shanks and serve immediately.

PREPARATION NOTES

If you prefer, you can substitute steaks or chops cut from the shoulder, which will reduce the cooking time of the meat to about 45 minutes. Like most braised foods, this dish will mellow and take on an even richer flavor if it is allowed to rest overnight in the refrigerator. Prepare the recipe through step 6. When you are ready to serve the dish, lift off any fat that may have congealed on the surface, and then complete the recipe.

SERVING SUGGESTIONS

Risotto, bowtie pasta, or barley pilaf would be go well with this dish. Serve with steamed seasonal vegetables to round out the meal.

Nutritional information per serving: 430 calories; 51 grams protein; 20 grams fat; 9 grams carbohydrate; 400 milligrams sodium; 157 milligrams cholesterol.

Lamb Chops with Sherry Vinegar Sauce

The procedure below calls for the lamb chops to be grilled, but if you prefer, they could just as easily be sautéed. The cooking time is approximately the same for both grilling and sautéing.

Makes 4 servings

4 lamb chops (cut from the rib)
2 teaspoons whole fresh rosemary leaves
¼ teaspoon cracked black peppercorns
2 teaspoons tightly-packed brown sugar
1 tablespoon sherry wine vinegar
1 tablespoon minced shallots
1½ cups chicken broth
1 teaspoon cornstarch

IN ADVANCE Preheat the grill or broiler.

1. Trim any visible fat from the chops and pat them dry with absorbent toweling. Rub the rosemary leaves and black peppercorns over both sides of the chops.

2. Heat the sugar, vinegar, and shallots in a saucepan over high heat. When the sugar is dissolved, add the broth and bring the sauce to a simmer.

3. Dilute the cornstarch in a teaspoon of cold water, then add it to the simmering sauce. Continue to simmer until the sauce is lightly thickened, about 2 to 3 minutes.

4. Keep the sauce warm over low heat while preparing the lamb chops.

5. Grill the lamb chops on one side for about 4 to 5 minutes, then turn the chops and continue to cook them to the desired doneness (another 3 to 4 minutes for medium).

6. Transfer the chops from the grill to heated plates or a serving platter.

7. Pour or ladle the sauce over the chops and serve at once.

PREPARATION NOTES

The sauce can be prepared through step 3, cooled, then refrigerated for up to 2 days. Be sure to bring it just to a boil, then quickly reduce the heat. Cornstarch-thickened sauces should not be boiled for extended periods.

SERVING SUGGESTIONS

Serve with a lentil or bean stew; a rice pilaf (see Wild and Brown Rice Pilaf with Cranberries, page 182) would also be a good choice. Steamed or sautéed spinach, escarole, broccoli, or asparagus could complete the meal.

Nutritional information per serving: 300 calories; 39 grams protein; 12 grams fat; 4 grams carbohydrate; 110 milligrams sodium; 120 milligrams cholesterol.

Calf's Liver, Berlin Style

The combination of apples and onions give this recipe a rich, unique flavor. The trick is to allow plenty of time for the onions to slowly cook to a rich golden brown.

Makes 4 servings

1½ pounds calf's liver, sliced
½ cup all-purpose flour
½ teaspoon salt
¼ teaspoon ground black pepper
1 tablespoon corn oil
2 yellow onions, sliced thin
1 Granny Smith apple, cored and sliced
½ cup chicken or beef broth

IN ADVANCE   Preheat the oven to 325°F.

1.   Trim the liver slices if necessary to remove any silverskin or gristle.

2.   In a shallow bowl, combine the flour with the salt and pepper. Dredge the liver in the flour and shake off any excess.

3.   Heat the oil in a nonstick or cast-iron skillet over high heat. Add the liver slices in a single layer. Do not crowd them; cook the slices one or two at a time, if necessary. Sear each slice on both sides. Place the slices on a baking sheet and finish cooking them in the oven. Remove the liver after 10 minutes and keep warm.

4.   Add the onion to the skillet and sauté over medium heat until they turn golden brown, for about 12 to 15 minutes.

5.   Add the sliced apple and sauté for another 3 to 4 minutes. Add the broth and simmer briefly. Taste and add salt and pepper to taste if necessary.

6.   Serve the liver on heated plates or a serving platter topped with the onion and apple mixture.

The liver must be cooked in hot oil, over high heat, to prevent it from turning an unappetizing gray. Be sure that the slices are about ½-inch thick; any thicker and it will be difficult to cook them properly. If desired, the liver can be given a light coating of breadcrumbs for a texture contrast.

SERVING SUGGESTIONS

A warm potato salad, a stew of grilled or roasted vegetables, or steamed broccoli with a light lemon glaze are good side-dish choices.

Nutritional information per serving: 460 calories; 44 grams protein; 22 grams fat; 18 grams carbohydrate; 440 milligrams sodium; 470 milligrams cholesterol.

Grains and Beans

5

Of the many benefits that have arisen from our growing concern with eating healthfully, one of the most obvious is the renewed (or new) acquaintance with the wealth of wonderful recipes for grains and legumes. Most ethnic cuisines have several examples of an intuitive "mutual supplementation," which provide not only the nutritional benefits of the complex carbohydrates and fiber found in grains and beans, but also a low-fat source of good-quality protein.

Most people are already familiar with rice. But even that old standby has been infused with a new excitement, as a variety of rices including brown, basmati or Texmati, Arborio, and wild rice, are featured in dishes on all sorts of menus. Brown rice is simply white rice that has not had the bran polished away. Basmati or Texmati rice (and other aromatic rices including "popcorn" or "pecan" rice) have a rich perfume that makes them especially delicious. Arborio rice is a special short-grain rice that, when stirred constantly as it cooks, develops a rich, creamy, porridge-like consistency while each separate kernel retains an individual "bite." The Venetians have raised the preparation of this dish to sublime heights by introducing such ingredients as saffron, Parmesan cheese, or shellfish. Wild rice, which is native to North America, is the seed of an aquatic grass, and has been cultivated and harvested by Native Americans tribes living in the Great Lakes region of the United States. Recently, however, commercial attempts at cultivating wild rice have been successful, making this once exotic grain more readily accessible.

Other grains, including cornmeal, couscous, barley, millet, quinoa, kasha, and bulgur, have joined rice on menus and supermarket shelves. Most of these grains cook quickly, few requiring more than 30 minutes. Some, notably bulgur and couscous, cook in 10 minutes or less. Grains have a subtle flavor that make them excellent accompaniments to a wide variety of foods. They can stand on their own, or they can readily adapt to a supporting role, easily carrying the flavors of other foods.

With the exception of the baked beans that almost invariably accompanied hot dogs and hamburgers at outdoor summer meals or a baked ham supper, dried beans, lentils, and peas had at one time practically disappeared from many kitchens across the nation. When Tex–Mex and Southwestern cooking became popular, beans came into their own. But it isn't just these two cooking styles that employ a variety of dried beans and peas. Any country or region with a rich "peasant" tradition has at least one bean dish in their repetoire.

While it is certainly fine to substitute one bean for another in many recipes, it is possible to taste a noticeable difference between favas and limas, black beans or kidney beans, and navy beans and black-eyed peas.

Different types of beans will require different cooking times. Lentils and split peas generally cook in about 30 to 45 minutes. On the other hand, chick peas and lima beans can take up to two hours. If your time is limited, use canned beans instead of cooking dried beans from scratch. Drain the beans and rinse them to remove the canning liquid. This will help reduce the sodium level in the finished dish.

When purchasing grains and dried beans, shop in stores whose business is relatively brisk, whether you prefer to buy them already packaged or from "bulk" bins. These foods do have an extended shelf life, but the older they are, the longer they take to cook, and the more liquid they may require. As they age, their flavor can also turn musty and stale. Keep whole grains in the refrigerator or freezer if you won't be using them within a few weeks of purchase. Beans, lentils, and dried peas can be stored in plastic bags or other storage containers for a few months, and don't require refrigeration.

Bulgur with Dried Cherries and Apples

The combination of the bulgur with dried fruit gives it a definite flavor boost, adding a sweet-tart taste. This dish is a good choice for rich, roasted meats, such as pork or duck.

Makes 4 to 6 servings

2 cups broth or *water*
¾ cups bulgur wheat
½ teaspoon salt
2 tablespoons coarsely chopped dried cherries
2 dried apple rings, coarsely chopped

1. Place the broth in a saucepan and bring to a boil over high heat.

2. Add the bulgur wheat to the boiling liquid and stir well with a fork to remove any lumps. Reduce the heat to low and simmer for about 3 to 4 minutes. Remove the pan from the heat.

3. Add the salt, cherries, and apples to the pan and fold in gently using a fork. Cover the pan and let rest for about 10 minutes before serving. This will allow the bulgur to absorb the flavors of the fruit.

PREPARATION NOTES

Bulgur is usually found along with other grains in larger supermarkets; otherwise, you can purchase it in bulk at many health food stores.

A somewhat unusual dried fruit, kiln-dried sour cherries are available in gourmet markets. If you prefer, use dried cranberries or blueberries instead.

SERVING SUGGESTIONS

This could be served as a hot breakfast cereal. If desired, sprinkle each serving with a little cinnamon sugar and top with a little warmed milk.

Nutritional information per serving: 200 calories; 7 grams protein; 1 gram fat; 42 grams carbohydrate; 145 milligrams sodium; less than 5 milligrams cholesterol.

Hoppin' John

Fresh black-eyed peas (also known as "cow peas" in some areas of the country) are available at certain times of the year, and can be substituted for the dried peas. Simply add the fresh peas to the rice during the last 10 minutes of cooking time; it's unnecessary to cook them separately in advance. You can also use canned black-eyed peas—just drain and rinse them first.

Makes 4 servings

½ cup dried black-eyed peas
1 to 1½ cups water
1 bacon strip, chopped
½ cup diced onion
2 garlic cloves, minced fine
¼ teaspoon red pepper flakes (or more to taste)
¾ cup long-grain rice
1¼ cups chicken broth
1 red or green bell pepper, seeded and diced
1 bay leaf
1 sprig of fresh thyme (or ½ teaspoon dried leaves)
¼ teaspoon salt (or to taste)
⅛ teaspoon freshly ground black pepper (or to taste)

1.   Place the black-eyed peas in a large pot and add enough cold water to cover by about 2 inches. Bring the water to a simmer over medium heat, and continue to cook until the peas are just tender, about 10 minutes for fresh black-eyed peas, or 30 minutes for dried peas. Drain them and reserve.

2.   Cook the bacon in a separate saucepan over medium heat, stirring frequently, until the bacon is crisp. Remove the bacon with a slotted spoon and drain it on absorbent toweling.

3. Pour off all but enough bacon fat to lightly coat the pan. Add the onion, garlic, and red pepper. Sauté over medium heat, stirring from time to time, until the onion turns golden brown.

4. Add the rice to the pan and sauté, stirring constantly, for another 2 minutes.

5. Add the chicken broth and bring the mixture to a boil. Add the drained black-eyed peas, bay leaf, and thyme. Cover the pot and cook over low heat or in a 325°F oven for 18 to 20 minutes, or until the rice is tender to the bite.

6. Remove the cover, fluff the Hoppin' John with a fork, and gently fold in the bacon pieces. Taste the mixture and adjust the seasoning with salt and pepper if needed. Serve with hot sauce.

PREPARATION NOTES

To convert this recipe to a vegetarian dish, make the following alterations: replace the bacon with 1 to 2 tablespoons of olive or peanut oil; increase the garlic to 3 cloves; use vegetable stock or water to replace the chicken stock.

SERVING SUGGESTIONS

• As part of a meatless entrée, pair this dish with sautéed greens (collard, mustard, kale, escarole, or spinach) that have been seasoned with plenty of pepper, garlic, and wilted onion. Add a dash of vinegar to the greens just before serving, or pass it on the side. Cornbread will round out the meal.

• This also makes an excellent accompaniment for grilled ham steaks, sausages, or baked catfish.

Nutritional information per serving: 230 calories; 9 grams protein; 5 grams fat; 39 grams carbohydrate; 160 milligrams sodium; 5 milligrams cholesterol.

Curried Braised Lentils with Eggplant and Mushrooms

Turmeric, one of the spices used in this dish, is a relative of ginger. It is used throughout tropical Asia and is a common ingredient in curry powders. The bright yellow color it imparts make it a good saffron substitute, but because of its tendency to overpower other flavors with its own earthy, slightly bitter flavor, it should be added with discretion. The Burmese are especially fond of adding this spice to vegetable dishes.

Makes 6 servings

1 cup green or brown lentils
4 cups broth or water
1 tablespoon olive oil
1 garlic clove, minced fine
1 teaspoon grated fresh ginger root
1 yellow onion, diced
2 cups diced eggplant
1 cup quartered mushrooms
1 teaspoon curry powder
1/4 teaspoon ground cinnamon
1/4 teaspoon ground turmeric
1 teaspoon lemon zest
1/2 teaspoon salt
1/4 teaspoon freshly ground black pepper

1. Place the lentils and the broth or water in a large pot and bring to a simmer over medium-high heat. Cook until the lentils are barely tender to the bite. Remove the pot from the heat and set aside, leaving the lentils in the cooking liquid, until needed.

2. Heat the oil in a skillet over medium heat. Add the garlic, ginger, and onion. Sauté, stirring occasionally, until the onion turns a light golden brown, about 6 to 8 minutes.

3. Add the eggplant, mushrooms, curry, cinnamon, turmeric, and lemon zest. Continue to cook, stirring occasionally, until the mushrooms begin to release some moisture, about 5 minutes.

4. Drain the lentils, reserving 1 cup of the cooking liquid, and combine them with the eggplant and mushroom mixture. Add enough of the cooking liquid to moisten well. Cover the skillet and cook over low heat until the eggplant is very tender, about 30 minutes. Add the salt and pepper and serve at once.

PREPARATION NOTES

This dish can be made in advance and refrigerated for up to 3 days or frozen for up to 6 weeks. Transfer to a casserole dish, coat with an even layer of fresh breadcrumbs, and drizzle with melted unsalted butter. Then place the casserole in a hot oven (400 to 425°F) for about 20 minutes, or until the dish is heated through and the crust is crisp and brown. If the crust is browning too quickly, cover the casserole with foil, then remove the foil during the last 5 minutes of cooking.

You can also use a microwave to reheat the lentils. The time will vary depending upon how much you are reheating; on average, 1 minute at full power is sufficient for a single serving.

SERVING SUGGESTIONS

• For a vegetarian banquet, serve these lentils with a selection of other items, such as steamed potatoes and new peas, fragrant basmati rice, chutneys, and sliced cucumbers dressed with mint, lemon, and yogurt.

• You can serve any leftover lentils cold, as a salad.

• Scoop out zucchini and yellow squash, fill with the lentils, bake until the squash is tender, and serve with a tomato sauce.

Nutritional information per serving: 170 calories; 12 grams protein; 4 grams fat; 25 grams carbohydrate; 190 milligrams sodium; less than 5 milligrams cholesterol.

Three Bean Stew

Combining a number of different beans in the same dish provides good color contrast, which will automatically make your plate look livelier. Adding brightly colored vegetables will further enhance this dish's visual appeal.

Makes 4 entrée or 6 to 8 side-dish servings

2 teaspoons olive oil
2 garlic cloves, finely minced
2 teaspoon minced shallots
1 celery stalk, finely diced
2 medium carrots, finely diced
1 yellow onion, finely diced
2 plum tomatoes, peeled, seeded, and chopped
1 tablespoon curry powder
½ teaspoon toasted cumin seed, ground
¾ cup kidney beans, cooked and drained
¾ cup black beans, cooked and drained
½ cup chick peas, cooked and drained
1 cup chicken or vegetable broth, or water
1 cup diced zucchini
¼ teaspoon cracked black peppercorns
1 tablespoon chopped fresh parsley
1 tablespoon chopped fresh cilantro
1 tablespoon chopped fresh mint
½ teaspoon salt (or to taste)

IN ADVANCE   Cook the beans separately until they are just tender to the bite. Drain and reserve.

1.   Heat the oil in a large, deep skillet over medium heat. Add the garlic, shallots, celery, carrots, and onion and sauté, stirring from time to time, until the onion takes on a light golden color, about 5 to 6 minutes.

2. Add the tomatoes and sauté for 2 to 3 minutes.

3. Add the curry and cumin and sauté for another 2 minutes.

4. Add the beans, broth, and zucchini. Increase the heat to high and bring the liquid to a boil. Reduce the heat to low, cover the pot, and simmer gently for 15 to 20 minutes. Check the stew periodically and add a little extra broth or water if necessary to keep the stew moist.

5. Add the pepper, parsley, cilantro, and mint. Add salt and pepper to taste and serve.

PREPARATION NOTES

Taste the stew after adding the pepper and herbs. To adjust the seasoning without adding salt, try one or more of the following: lemon juice, a few drops of tamari or reduced-sodium soy sauce, balsamic vinegar, or Tabasco sauce.

Feel free to substitute different beans for those recommended here. Fava or lima beans are excellent, but remember to peel them unless they are fresh baby beans. Use canned beans for a quick version of this recipe, but rinse them before adding to the stew.

SERVING SUGGESTIONS

For a meat-free dinner, serve this stew with a rice pilaf or a wedge of cornbread.

Nutritional information per serving: 140 calories; 9 grams protein; 1 grams fat; 23 grams carbohydrate; 5 milligrams sodium; trace of cholesterol.

Southwest White Bean Stew

The heat in this dish comes from fresh jalapeños, a chile that ranks a score of 5.5 on the Scoville scale—a rating of the relative heat or mildness of chiles. That score places jalapeños in the "medium hot" category. The hottest chiles, with a score of 10, are habañeros and their relatives—pequins and the Scotch bonnet. For extra pungence and a smoky flavor, use canned chipotle chiles packed in adobo sauce, to taste.

Makes 4 main-course or 6 to 8 side-dish servings

2 cups cooked, drained navy beans
2 teaspoons vegetable oil
1 small red onion, diced
1 bell pepper (green, red, or yellow), diced
1 to 2 teaspoons minced jalapeños
2 garlic cloves, minced
3 tablespoons sherry wine vinegar
1 plum tomato (fresh or canned), peeled, seeded, and chopped
1 tablespoon chopped fresh cilantro
¼ teaspoon ground black pepper (or to taste)

IN ADVANCE Cook navy beans in simmering water or broth until just barely tender to the bite. Drain the beans before measuring them.

1. Puree about half of the cooked beans in a food processor or blender, and then combine with the remaining whole beans.

2. Heat the oil in a skillet over medium heat. Add the onion, bell pepper, jalapeños, and garlic. Sauté, stirring frequently, until the onion becomes translucent, about 5 to 6 minutes.

3. Add the bean mixture and sauté, stirring constantly, until the beans are heated through, about 5 minutes.

4. Add the vinegar and tomato, and simmer for another 8 to 10 minutes. Stir frequently, and add a small amount of water if the stew seems too thick.

5. Add the cilantro and pepper and adjust the seasoning to taste if needed just before serving with additional salt, pepper, or vinegar.

PREPARATION NOTES

For a slightly different taste, texture, and presentation, replace the navy beans with pinto beans, cranberry beans, or Great Northern beans. To add color to the mix, add a few tablespoons of red lentils in step 4.

SERVING SUGGESTIONS

• This stew makes an excellent backdrop for grilled salmon, swordfish, or tuna.

• It also can be used as a filling for burritos or enchiladas.

• To convert this dish into a meat-free main course, serve with a whole-grain pasta such as fusilli, elbow macaroni, or penne.

Nutritional information per serving: 160 calories; 8 grams protein; 2 grams fat; 28 grams carbohydrate; 180 milligrams sodium; trace of cholesterol.

Hush Puppies

No one is really sure where this dish originated, or how it earned its name. One story tells it this way: Fishermen would drop spoonfuls of the batter they used to fry their catches into hot oil. Once cooked, the fishermen fed these little nuggets to their dogs to keep them quiet.

Makes 4 servings

1 cup yellow cornmeal
½ teaspoon salt
¼ teaspoon freshly ground black pepper
1 teaspoon baking powder
1 cup milk
1 whole egg, lightly beaten
2 tablespoons melted unsalted butter
2 tablespoons chopped scallions
vegetable oil as needed for deep frying

IN ADVANCE Preheat vegetable oil to 375°F. A 1-inch cube of bread added to oil at the correct temperature will brown in 50 seconds at 375°F.

1. Combine the cornmeal, salt, pepper, and baking powder in a bowl. Blend to distribute the baking powder evenly. Set aside.

2. Beat together the milk, egg, butter, and scallions in a small bowl. Add this mixture to the cornmeal and stir just until blended.

3. Use a soup spoon to drop the batter into the hot oil. Fry the hush puppies until they are puffed up and golden brown on all sides.

4. Lift the hush puppies from the hot oil with a spider or a frying basket. Drain briefly on absorbent toweling, then serve at once.

Add diced green or red peppers, bacon bits, or grated cheese to the batter before frying if desired.

• Hush puppies are traditionally served as an accompaniment to fried fish, but they also go well with fried or baked chicken.

• To serve as a breakfast dish, omit the scallions and pass with a little maple syrup on the side.

Nutritional information per serving: 210 calories; 3 grams protein; 12 grams fat; 21 grams carbohydrate; 190 milligrams sodium; 20 milligrams cholesterol.

Timbales of Dirty Rice

In the traditional Cajun version of this dish, chicken livers, gizzards, and necks would be simmered until tender in a broth, diced, and added to the rice. This version, featured at St. Andrew's Café, significantly reduces calories, fat, cholesterol, and sodium.

Makes 4 servings

½ cup fresh cranberry beans
1 cup chicken broth
½ cup minced onions
2 garlic cloves, finely minced
½ cup converted long-grain rice
1 tablespoon tomato paste
1 tablespoon cider vinegar
2 to 3 drops Tabasco sauce
1 teaspoon chopped jalapeños
½ teaspoon cumin seeds, toasted
½ teaspoon freshly ground black pepper
½ teaspoon paprika
cayenne pepper to taste
¼ cup grated aged cheddar cheese
½ cup corn kernels

IN ADVANCE Preheat the oven to 375°F, if you wish to cook the rice mixture in the oven.

1. Simmer the cranberry beans in water until they are tender enough to mash easily with a fork. (Cooking time will depend upon the age of the beans.) Drain the beans, mash them lightly with a fork, and set aside.

2. Heat 2 tablespoons of the broth in a saucepan, then add the onions and garlic. Cover the pan and allow the onion to smother in the broth over low heat for about 5 minutes.

3. Add the rice to the mixture and cook, stirring constantly, for 2 minutes.

4. Add the remaining broth, tomato paste, vinegar, Tabasco, jalapeños, cumin, pepper, paprika, and cayenne. Stir the mixture with a kitchen fork and bring to barely a simmer over medium heat.

5. Cover the pot and cook on the stovetop over low heat or in a 325°F oven for 16 to 18 minutes, or until the rice is tender to the bite.

6. Fluff the rice with a kitchen fork to release any steam. Fold the mashed beans, cheese, and corn into the rice with the kitchen fork, and serve at once.

PREPARATION NOTES

If fresh cranberry beans are not available, substitute cooked or canned red kidney beans that have been drained and rinsed.

For a vegetarian dish, omit the cheese and replace the chicken broth with vegetable broth or water.

SERVING SUGGESTIONS

Make this dish the centerpiece of a meatless meal by serving a variety of vegetables around the rice: grilled eggplant and summer squashes, steamed carrots and green beans, fresh asparagus tips, and okra sautéed with tomatoes.

Nutritional information per serving: 165 calories; 7 grams protein; 3 grams fat; 28 grams carbohydrate; 70 milligrams sodium; 10 milligrams cholesterol.

Quinoa Pilaf with Red and Yellow Peppers

Though quinoa (pronounced "KEEN-wah") is a relative newcomer to our markets, it is one of the more ancient New-World grains. When properly cooked, quinoa is light and fluffy with a subtle nutty flavor.

Makes 6 servings

2 cups chicken broth
1 tablespoon minced shallots
1 garlic clove, minced fine
⅔ cup quinoa
1 small bay leaf
1 sprig fresh thyme (or ½ teaspoon dried)
½ cup diced roasted red pepper
½ cup diced roasted yellow pepper
¼ teaspoon salt
¼ teaspoon freshly ground black pepper

IN ADVANCE   To roast peppers, use *one* of the following methods:

• Hold the pepper in the flame of a gas burner until blackened on all surfaces.

• Halve the peppers, place cut side down on a baking sheet, and broil until well-blackened.

• Grill the peppers over hot coals or on a gas grill. Once the skin is evenly charred, place the pepper in a paper bag and close tightly. Let steam for several minutes, then remove from the bag and scrape away the skin.

1.   Heat 2 tablespoons of the broth in a saucepan over medium heat. Add the shallots and garlic, and sauté them in the broth for 2 or 3 minutes, stirring frequently.

2. Add the quinoa, the remaining broth, bay leaf, and thyme. Stir well with a kitchen fork, and bring the mixture to a simmer over medium heat.

3. Reduce the heat to low, cover the pot, and simmer the quinoa for about 15 minutes, or until the quinoa is tender and very fluffy.

4. Remove and discard the bay leaf and thyme sprig. Fluff the grains with a fork to break up any clumps, and fold in the roasted peppers.

5. Taste to check the seasoning and add the salt and pepper if necessary. Serve at once.

PREPARATION NOTES

This dish may be prepared in the oven instead of on a burner. If you already have the oven on, just cook the quinoa along with whatever else is baking. As long as the temperature is at least 300°F and no more than 375°F, the quinoa will cook properly. Check the pilaf after about 12 minutes if the oven is set at more than 325°F; it may cook a little faster at a higher temperature.

SERVING SUGGESTIONS

Any leftover quinoa could be combined with diced vegetables such as cucumber, carrot, celery, avocado, and tomato, then dressed with a vinaigrette. Serve chilled as a salad, or as the filling for a pita sandwich garnished with alfalfa and radish sprouts.

Nutritional information per serving: 125 calories; 9 grams protein; 3 grams fat; 22 grams carbohydrate; 140 milligrams sodium; less than 5 milligrams cholesterol.

Lemon Cilantro Rice

Rice, with its subtle flavor, is an excellent vehicle to carry other flavors. The bright, sharp flavor of cilantro, a fresh herb common in Thai, Vietnamese, Chinese, and Mexican cooking, blends well with the tang of the lemon.

Makes 6 servings

1 tablespoon vegetable oil
1 medium onion, minced
zest and juice of 1 lemon (see Preparation Notes)
2 cups converted long-grain rice
4 cups chicken broth
3 to 4 tablespoons chopped fresh cilantro leaves
salt and freshly ground pepper to taste

1. Heat the oil over medium heat in a saucepot. Add the onion and sauté, stirring frequently, until it is limp and translucent.

2. Add the lemon zest and the rice. Stir to coat the rice evenly with the oil.

3. Add the broth and bring the mixture to a boil, then cover the pot with a tight-fitting lid. Continue to cook the rice over low heat on the stovetop, or transfer the pot to the oven and cook at 325°F, for about 18 to 20 minutes.

4. Remove the lid from the pot and fluff the rice with a fork. Remove the zest. Drizzle the lemon juice over the rice and add the chopped cilantro, using the fork to gently fold them into the rice.

5. Taste the rice and adjust the seasoning if necessary with salt and pepper.

Use a swivel-bladed peeler to cut away thin strips of lemon zest, without removing any of the bitter white pith beneath. The zest can be left in large pieces so that it is easy to find and discard after cooking. Be sure to remove the zest *before* squeezing the juice from the lemon.

You can choose the herbs for this recipe to complement other dishes served during the meal. Use fresh mint, oregano, thyme, dill, parsley, or chives, either individually or in any combination.

SERVING SUGGESTIONS

To make a ring of rice, place a cup or glass in the center of the plate and spoon the rice around it. Fill the center of the ring with a stew for a quick, attractive presentation.

Nutritional information per serving: 130 calories; 4 grams protein; 1 gram fat; 23 grams carbohydrate; 10 milligrams sodium; trace of cholesterol.

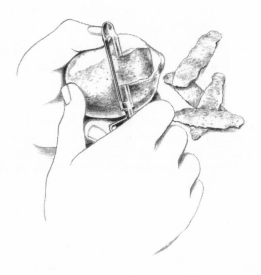

Polenta with Parmesan Cheese

A coarse-grained, stone-ground cornmeal (either white or yellow) will produce a polenta with a very robust "corn" flavor. Imported *Parmigiano Reggiano* is worth searching out for any dish requiring Parmesan cheese.

Makes 6 servings

3 tablespoons unsalted butter (plus additional for frying)
1 tablespoon minced shallots
1 garlic clove, minced fine
7 cups broth or water
1 teaspoon salt
1²⁄₃ cup cornmeal, yellow or white
1 egg yolk, lightly beaten
¼ cup grated Parmesan cheese

1. Heat the butter in a large saucepan. Add the shallots and garlic, and sauté over medium heat until the shallots are tender and translucent.

2. Add the broth and salt and bring the mixture to a rolling boil. Place the cornmeal in a pitcher and pour it into the boiling liquid in a thin stream, stirring constantly with a wooden spoon, until it has all been incorporated.

3. Reduce the heat to low, and stir constantly for about 2 minutes. Then, let the polenta cook, stirring for a full minute at 5-minute intervals. The total cooking time for polenta is about 40 to 45 minutes, and is properly cooked when the mixture forms a mass that pulls cleanly away from the sides of the pot.

4. Remove the polenta from the heat, and stir in the egg yolk and Parmesan. (Note: The polenta can be served at this point, while it is still soft and spoonable.)

5. Pour the polenta into a lightly greased baking dish and spread into an even layer. Cool the polenta completely, then refrigerate for several hours (be sure to wrap it well).

6.   Cut the polenta into wedges and panfry the pieces in butter over high heat until golden on both sides and heated through. Serve at once.

PREPARATION NOTES

There are a number of other delicious ways to serve polenta. It can be stuffed and baked, grilled, or broiled, and served with a sauce.

To make a very simple polenta, omit the first step and cook the cornmeal in boiling salted water, a mixture of stock and water, or a mixture of milk and water. Be careful when working with milk, as it tends to scorch easily. It is also fine to eliminate the egg yolk and Parmesan cheese if you're cutting fat and calories.

Polenta can be stored in the refrigerator for up to 3 days, as long as it is properly covered.

SERVING SUGGESTIONS

• Polenta makes an excellent accompaniment to grilled fish, meats, and poultry.

If you plan to serve polenta as an appetizer try one of the following:

• Slice the polenta and top it with a selection of wild mushrooms sautéed with a dash of wine, some heavy cream, and a generous amount of freshly ground pepper.

• Top the panfried polenta with grilled shrimp.

• Slice the polenta, layer it with crumbled gorgonzola cheese, and bake.

Nutritional information per serving: 235 calories; 10 grams protein; 10 grams fat; 27 grams carbohydrate; 480 milligrams sodium; 65 milligrams cholesterol.

Risotto with Asparagus Tips

Arborio is a special type of short-grain Italian rice that develops a soft, creamy texture when it is stirred constantly during cooking. Other types of rice can be used in this dish, but it will not have the special consistency associated with authentic risotto.

Makes 4 servings

1 pound fresh asparagus
3 tablespoons unsalted butter
½ cup onion, finely minced
1 cup Arborio rice
2 cups chicken broth, heated
½ cup dry white wine
¼ cup Parmesan cheese, freshly grated
½ teaspoon salt
¼ teaspoon freshly ground black pepper

IN ADVANCE Cut the tips from the asparagus (about 2 inches from the top) and cook for about 3 to 4 minutes in boiling salted water. Drain, rinse in cold water, and set aside.

1. Heat the butter in a saucepan over medium heat. Add the onion and sauté, stirring frequently, until it is quite tender, for about 5 minutes. Do not allow it to brown.

2. Add the rice and stir well to coat each grain with the butter.

3. Add about ½ cup of the stock and simmer, stirring constantly, until the liquid has nearly cooked away. Repeat this process, adding ½ cup of the stock at a time, until all of the stock has been added.

4. Add the wine and cook the risotto, stirring constantly, until the rice has absorbed the wine, is tender to the bite, and has a smooth, creamy consistency. The total cooking time will be about 15 to 20 minutes.

5. Remove the risotto from the heat and stir in the cheese, salt, pepper, and blanched asparagus tips. Serve at once.

PREPARATION NOTES

The "proper" way to prepare and serve risotto is to have the diners assembled and ready so that once it is finished cooking it can be served directly from the pot. If you need a little more flexibility, make the risotto accommodate your schedule: Incorporate all but the last ½ cup of liquid (in this recipe, the wine), then pour the risotto into a baking dish. Spread it into an even layer, let cool, then refrigerate for several hours. When you are ready, put the risotto back into a pot, add the wine, and simmer for another 5 minutes.

SERVING SUGGESTIONS

• Risotto can either be served in place of the pasta course in a traditional Italian dinner, or it can become the entire meal. Simply add fish or seafood (small pieces of raw halibut, turbot, or cod; peeled shrimp; clams or the lobster) during the last 10 to 12 minutes of cooking.

• For a vegetable risotto, add leeks, wild mushrooms, and diced or julienned fennel or celery root along with the onion in step 1. Or add shredded raw escarole or spinach, new peas, or blanched broccoli florets instead of the asparagus in step 5.

Nutritional information per serving: 315 calories; 10 grams protein; 11 grams fat; 44 grams carbohydrate; 450 milligrams sodium; 30 milligrams cholesterol.

Wild and Brown Rice Pilaf with Cranberries

Kiln-dried fruits, including cranberries, blueberries, sour cherries, and blackberries, are harvested when fully ripe and then quickly dried at very high temperatures to preserve the fullest flavor. They lend a unique taste that is both sweet and tart. Look for them in specialty shops, mail-order catalogs, or the international section of larger supermarkets.

Makes 4 servings

¼ *cup dried cranberries*
½ *cup apple cider*
2¾ *cups chicken broth*
¼ *cup minced onions*
½ *cup long-grain brown rice*
½ *cup wild rice*
¼ *teaspoon salt*
¼ *teaspoon freshly ground black pepper*

IN ADVANCE Place the cranberries and cider in a small saucepan and warm over low heat for 5 minutes. (You can also heat the cranberries and cider in a microwave oven for 40 seconds at full power.) Allow the cranberries to "plump" off the heat for about 10 minutes. Drain, reserving the cider.

1. Heat about ¼ cup of the broth in a saucepan over medium heat. Add the onions and sauté them, stirring frequently, until tender and translucent, about 4 to 5 minutes.

2. Add the brown and wild rices, the remaining broth, and the reserved cider. Bring the mixture to a simmer, cover the pot, and cook on the stovetop over low heat or in a 350°F oven for about 40 minutes, or until the rice is tender to the bite.

3. Fluff the rice with a kitchen fork to release the steam and break up any clumps. Add the drained cranberries and fold them into the rice mixture. Season with the salt and pepper.

PREPARATION NOTES

If you prepare this dish with white instead of brown rice, you would need to cook the wild rice separately, since it takes about 35 minutes to cook.

To use leftover cooked rice, follow the recipe through step 1, then add the cooked rice (any combination of white and brown rice, long-grain and short-grain, or wild rices is fine), cider, cranberries, and seasonings. Add ⅓ cup of broth and reheat until the rices are very hot.

SERVING SUGGESTIONS

• Pilaf complements grilled and roasted entrées well. Try it with roasted venison or pork and grilled salmon or tuna.

• As the centerpiece of a meatless meal, serve it with braised leeks or fennel, broiled tomato slices topped with garlic and fresh herbs, and a sauté of cauliflower and red peppers.

Nutritional information per serving: 215 calories; 8 grams protein; 2 grams fat; 44 grams carbohydrate; 145 milligrams sodium; less than 5 milligrams cholesterol.

Couscous with Wild Mushrooms and Walnuts

Couscous cooks so quickly that it can be prepared in the same amount of time as "instant" rice. It is not really a grain; couscous is actually a grain-shaped pasta, made from semolina wheat. A whole-wheat version can sometimes be found in health food stores.

Makes 4 servings

2 cups broth or water
1 teaspoon oil or butter (optional)
1 cup couscous
¼ teaspoon salt
½ cup sliced wild mushrooms (such as shiitake, boletus, or cêpes), or
   ¼ cup dried wild mushrooms
1 teaspoon grated orange zest
2 tablespoons coarsely chopped toasted walnuts

IN ADVANCE If you are using dried wild mushrooms, reconstitute them by pouring enough boiling water over them to cover completely. Let soak for about 15 minutes, drain, and use as you would fresh mushrooms.

1. Place the broth or water (along with the oil or butter, if using) in a saucepan and bring to a boil over high heat.

2. Add the couscous to the boiling liquid and stir well with a fork to remove any lumps. Return to a boil, then remove the pan from the heat.

3. Add the salt, mushrooms, and orange zest to the pan, and fold in gently using a fork. Cover the pan and allow it to rest for about 5 minutes before serving.

4. Using two forks, gently fluff the couscous with a lifting or tossing motion, taking care to break up any lumps. Serve topped with the toasted walnuts.

To give the couscous's cooking liquid a more robust flavor, strain the dried mushrooms' soaking liquid through a coffee filter and use it in place of part of the broth or water.

If you can't find fresh or dried wild mushrooms, sliced domestic mushrooms are an acceptable substitute.

SERVING SUGGESTIONS

Couscous makes a wonderful base for savory vegetable stews or curries, or as a side dish with grilled lamb or pan-seared fish.

Nutritional information per serving: 95 calories; 4 grams protein; 2 grams fat; 17 grams carbohydrate; 70 milligrams sodium; trace of cholesterol.

Kasha with Spicy Maple Pecans

Kasha is toasted and coarsely cracked buckwheat with a delicious nutty aroma and taste. It can be found in most supermarkets along with other grains. If you have trouble locating it, look for the words "buckwheat groats" on the box's label.

Makes 6 servings

1 egg white, lightly beaten
¾ cup kasha
2 cups broth or water
¼ teaspoon salt
1 teaspoon butter (optional)
¼ cup toasted pecans, chopped
2 tablespoons maple syrup
pinch of cayenne pepper (or to taste)

1. Combine the egg white and kasha in a saucepan and cook over low heat, stirring constantly, for 2 minutes.

2. Add the broth or water, salt, and butter to the kasha and bring to a boil over high heat. Reduce the heat to low and simmer the kasha, covered, for about 15 minutes.

3. Keeping the pan covered, remove the kasha from the heat and allow it to absorb the remaining liquid for about 5 minutes.

4. Place the pecans, maple syrup, and cayenne in a small skillet. Cook over low heat until the pecans are well-coated and the maple syrup is reduced to a very thick consistency.

5. Remove the lid from the kasha and, using two forks, fluff it with a lifting or tossing motion, taking care to break up any lumps. Scatter the spiced pecans over the kasha and serve.

Kasha must first be coated with egg white in order to prevent it from lumping as it cooks. Other grains, such as white or brown rice or pearl barley, could also be prepared using this recipe; simply omit the first step of sautéing them in the egg white. The cooking times would be 16 minutes for white rice, 35 minutes for brown rice, and 25 minutes for pearl barley.

SERVING SUGGESTIONS

• Kasha with roasted chicken or turkey, or broiled bluefish or marlin.

• For a vegetarian feast, serve the kasha with cabbage rolls stuffed with vegetables and simmered in tomato sauce, steamed fresh asparagus or peas, glazed carrots, and pickled beets.

Nutritional information per serving: 135 calories; 5 grams protein; 4 grams fat; 22 grams carbohydrate; 100 milligrams sodium; trace of cholesterol.

Lentil Ragout

There are many different types of lentils. Green or brown lentils are most readily available in grocery stores. If possible, try to locate French lentils. They are plumper than ordinary lentils, hold their shape better during cooking, and have a rich nutty flavor.

Makes 6 servings

1 bacon strip, finely chopped
1 yellow onion, finely diced
1 carrot, finely diced
1 celery stalk, finely diced
1 garlic clove, finely minced
2 tablespoons tomato paste
1 cup green or brown lentils
2½ cups chicken or vegetable broth
1 bay leaf
1 sprig fresh thyme (or ½ teaspoon dried)
1 strip of lemon zest
1 to 2 tablespoons sherry wine vinegar
¼ teaspoon coarsely cracked black peppercorns
¼ teaspoon salt

1. Place the bacon in a saucepan and cook over medium heat until the fat is released and the bacon is crisp. Remove the bacon with a slotted spoon and set aside.

2. Add the onion, carrot, celery, and garlic to the fat left in the pan. Cover and cook the vegetables over low heat without stirring, for about 5 to 6 minutes, or until the onion is very limp.

3. Remove the cover and add the tomato paste. Raise the heat to high and sauté, stirring constantly, for about 3 minutes.

4. Add the lentils, broth, bay leaf, thyme, and lemon zest. Reduce the heat to low and simmer, stirring occasionally, until the lentils are tender, about 30 minutes. (The lentils may also be cooked, tightly covered, in a 350°F oven for about 45 minutes.)

5. Remove and discard the bay leaf, thyme sprig, and lemon peel. Add the vinegar to taste. Taste and add the salt and pepper if needed. Serve at once.

PREPARATION NOTES

To prepare a vegetarian version of the ragout, substitute a tablespoon of olive oil for the bacon.

This dish can be refrigerated for up to 3 days or frozen for up to 8 weeks. Bring it to a full boil when reheating it and check the seasoning. Add more vinegar, salt, or pepper if needed.

SERVING SUGGESTIONS

• Pool the ragout on heated plates to act as a sauce for grilled fish or chicken, or add it to the Braised Lamb Shanks (see page 00) during the last 15 minutes of cooking time.

• For a hearty main-course soup or stew, thin the finished dish with some additional stock and add a variety of diced cooked vegetables.

• To serve this dish as a vegetarian entrée, ladle the finished ragout over basmati rice, barley, or couscous, and accompany it with a variety of steamed or boiled seasonal vegetables and a crisp green salad.

Nutritional information per serving: 160 calories; 10 grams protein; 4 grams fat; 24 grams carbohydrate; 115 milligrams sodium; 5 milligrams cholesterol.

Wild Rice Pancakes

Wild rice is graded according to the length of the individual grain. Shorter, or broken, grains cost less than whole long-grain wild rice. If you have the option, choose the less expensive wild rice since a uniform grain is not as important for the dish's appearance as it would be in a pilaf.

Makes 8 servings

1 cup wild rice
3 cups chicken broth
1 teaspoon chopped garlic
1 medium onion, grated
1 medium red pepper, finely diced
2 whole eggs, lightly beaten
1½ to 2 cups all-purpose flour
½ teaspoon salt (or to taste)
¼ teaspoon freshly ground black pepper (or more to taste)
2 tablespoons oil or
2 tablespoons clarified butter

1. In a large saucepan, simmer the wild rice in the broth until it is tender, about 40 to 45 minutes. If all of the stock is absorbed before the rice is cooked, add more broth or water to prevent scorching.

2. To speed cooling, turn the rice out of the pan into a shallow baking dish and spread into an even layer.

3. Combine the rice, garlic, onion, red pepper, and eggs in a large bowl and blend well.

4. Add enough flour to make a heavy batter, slightly thicker than a pancake batter. Season to taste with salt and pepper.

5. Over medium heat in a heavy skillet, place enough oil and clarified butter to cover the pan by about ⅛ inch.

6. Drop the batter by soup-spoonfuls into the skillet and flatten to form pancakes about ¼-inch thick. Cook on one side for about 2 minutes, then turn the pancakes and cook for 2 minutes more, until golden and crisp. Remove the cakes from the pan and drain briefly on absorbent toweling. Serve at once. If necessary, place the pancakes in an uncovered ovenproof dish and keep warm in a 200°F oven until ready to serve.

PREPARATION NOTES

To clarify butter, cut whole butter into pieces and place in a saucepan or microwaveable container. Heat over moderate heat or in the microwave until the butter melts and separates into layers. There will be a small amount of foam on the surface, a clear liquid (the clarified butter) in the middle, and milk solids and water on the bottom. Skim the foam from the surface of the butter, and then carefully ladle away the clear liquid. Discard the milky liquid that has settled at the bottom of the container. To reduce or elminate cooking fat, use a non-stick skillet.

SERVING SUGGESTIONS

• Served with apple sauce, cranberry relish, or sour cream, these crunchy pancakes make an excellent accompaniment to sautéed or poached fish, grilled turkey steaks, or baked chicken.

• For a wonderful savory appetizer, try topping the pancakes with sour cream or crème fraîche and slivers of *prosciutto* or smoked salmon.

Nutritional information per serving: 220 calories; 9 grams protein; 5 grams fat; 34 grams carbohydrate; 180 milligrams sodium; 75 milligrams cholesterol.

Vegetables

6

With the increased distribution of locally and regionally grown produce, there are more vegetables available to the home cook than ever before. The recipes in this chapter offer a wide range of choices for those who are eager to expand their repertoire of vegetable dishes. Many offer suggestions that would make it possible to create vegetarian meals with one or two selections.

Always keep in mind when working with vegetables that they are, in general, highly perishable. As soon as any vegetable is harvested, it begins to undergo some significant changes, and the more perishable the vegetable, the more dramatic the change. Sweet corn and peas, for instance, begin converting sugars into starch immediately after picking, giving over-the-hill corn and peas that telltale sticky texture and pasty taste. Other vegetables also continue to age, wilt, and soften after harvesting, and when you add on the time that it takes to transport the produce from the fields to market, you can see why it is best to cook vegetables as soon as possible after purchasing them in order to preserve their fresh taste and vibrant colors. The more delicious, fresh, and appealing a vegetable looks before it is cooked, the greater the level of nutrients.

Root vegetables (sometimes called winter vegetables) have a longer shelf life, and can generally be stored without any significant loss of quality for weeks, and with careful handling, even months. Hard-skinned squashes, turnips, parsnips, carrots, and cabbages can also be stored for longer periods. A constant cool temperature, a relatively high-moisture content in the air, and a good covering of hay or straw are the best strategies for their extended storage. Most of us don't have root cellars, though, so it is best to use these vegetables within a week or two of purchasing them.

There are no recipes in this chapter for simply steamed or boiled vegetables. To use these basic techniques as well as those found in our recipes, just remember the following rules:

1. Use the freshest produce available.

2. Peel, rinse, and/or cut as close to cooking time as possible.

3. To help retain the water-soluble vitamins, use as little cooking liquid as possible. Steaming, cooking in the microwave, or baking whole with the skins on are all good options.

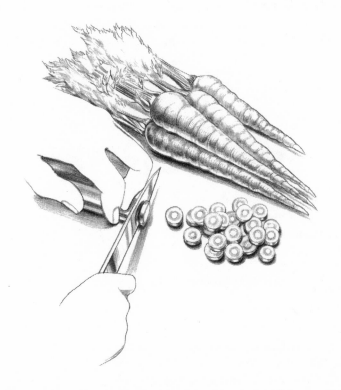

4. When steaming or boiling vegetables, cook them just until tender to the bite. The color should be a bright, appealing shade, with no dull gray or yellow tones for green or white vegetables.

5. Serve the vegetables as soon as you can, once they have been cooked.

The liquid used to steam or boil many vegetables can be saved and used in place of chicken or vegetable broth in other recipes, or added to soups, broths, and stews. Just taste the broth to be sure that the flavor is fresh and appealing. Strongly flavored vegetables (certain members of the cabbage family, such as turnips, rutabagas, and beets, for instance) may not be suitable.

Carrot Timbales

These timbales are a healthful version of a classic vegetable dish. The original version incorporated heavy cream and egg yolks. You'll find that even without these high-fat ingredients, the end result is suave and deceptively creamy.

Makes 6 timbales

2 teaspoons vegetable oil
¼ cup finely minced onions
2 teaspoons finely minced shallots
4 carrots, peeled and coarsely chopped
½ cup vegetable or chicken broth
1 small bay leaf
2 parsley stems
2 egg whites
⅓ cup evaporated skim milk
⅛ teaspoon salt
⅛ teaspoon ground white pepper

1.   Heat 1 teaspoon of the oil in a skillet over medium heat. Add the onion and shallots and cook over low to medium heat until limp but not browned.

2.   Add the carrots, broth, bay leaf, and parsley stems. Cover and simmer over low heat until the carrots are very tender and most of the broth has cooked away.

3.   Remove the mixture from the heat and discard the bay leaf and parsley stems. Let cool slightly, then puree the carrots in a food processor or blender until they are smooth. Transfer the mixture to a bowl and allow it to cool to room temperature.

4.   In a separate bowl, blend the egg whites, milk, salt, and pepper. Add this mixture to the carrots.

5.   Spray or brush 2-ounce timbales or soufflé molds with the remaining oil. Spoon the carrot mixture into the molds, leaving about ½ inch of space at the top. Place the filled molds in a deep baking dish.

6.   Place the pan on the oven rack, then add enough boiling water so that it meets the level of the vegetable mixture in the molds. Cover the molds with a sheet of waxed or parchment paper and bake for about 18 to 20 minutes, or until the timbales are set and a paring knife inserted in the center of a mold comes out clean.

7.   Unmold the timbales onto heated plates and serve at once.

PREPARATION NOTES

You can use this recipe to prepare other vegetables, including broccoli, spinach, beets, or squash. Combinations of vegetables, such as parsnips and carrots or beets and acorn squash, would also make interesting variations.

SERVING SUGGESTIONS

• The timbales can be served as an accompaniment to a grilled or roasted entrée.

• To feature as an appetizer, serve with a red pepper coulis, a salsa, or a fresh tomato sauce.

Nutritional information: 60 calories; 3 grams protein; 1 gram fat; 10 grams carbohydrate; 104 milligrams sodium; trace of cholesterol.

Ratatouille

Ratatouille is one of the most famous European vegetable dishes. In the tradition of all great stews, it is perfectly admissable to add a little more of this, a little less of that, or whatever is at the peak of its season at the market. Cooking the garlic, onion, and tomato paste long enough to release their wonderful aromas will assure the success of the dish.

Makes 6 servings

2 tablespoons olive oil
2 teaspoons finely minced shallots
2 garlic cloves, minced
1 red onion, sliced thin
2 tablespoons tomato paste
2 cups diced eggplant
1 cup sliced zucchini
1 cup sliced yellow squash
1 cup diced bell pepper (green or red)
3 plum tomatoes, peeled, seeded, and chopped
2 tablespoons chopped fresh herbs (one or more of these: chives, parsley,
    tarragon, chervil, basil, oregano, rosemary)
½ teaspoon salt
¼ teaspoon freshly ground black pepper

1. Heat the olive oil in a skillet over medium heat. Add the shallots, garlic, and red onion. Sauté, stirring from time to time, for about 5 to 6 minutes, or until the onion is tender and translucent.

2. Add the tomato paste and cook briefly until it has a slightly rusty color and a sweet aroma.

3. Add the eggplant, zucchini, yellow squash, pepper, and tomatoes and stir well to combine.

4. Reduce the heat to establish a gentle simmer. Stew the vegetables, uncovered, until they are very tender, about 20 minutes.

5. Add the herbs, salt, and pepper. Serve at once.

PREPARATION NOTES

This recipe can be prepared in advance through step 4. Once cooled, the ratatouille can be refrigerated for up to 3 days or frozen for up to 2 months. Reheat thoroughly either on the stovetop or in the microwave. If you use the microwave, the heating time will vary greatly, depending upon the type of oven as well as the amount of ratatouille. Break the heating time down into smaller intervals, stirring well in between so that the vegetables are heated evenly.

For the best flavor, add the chopped fresh herbs just before serving.

SERVING SUGGESTIONS

• As the centerpiece of a vegetarian meal, serve the ratatouille with noodles, rice, or other grains. For additional protein, add cooked chick peas or other beans.

• For a richer flavor, add an ounce or two of chopped sun-dried tomatoes and top each serving with crumbled fresh goat cheese.

Nutritional information per serving: 80 calories; 2 grams protein; 5 grams fat; 10 grams carbohydrate; 190 milligrams sodium; 0 milligrams cholesterol.

Zucchini Stuffed with Mushrooms and Fennel

Use a very sharp knife or the slicing edge of your box grater to cut the fennel. If fennel is not available, substitute celery.

Makes 4 servings

2 medium zucchini, halved lengthwise and seeds removed
salt and freshly ground pepper to taste
freshly squeezed lemon juice to taste
3 tablespoons chopped chives
2 tablespoons olive oil
2 to 3 scallions, sliced thinly on the bias
1 clove garlic, finely minced
1 cup wild or domestic mushrooms, sliced
½ cup fennel, shaved or thinly sliced
2 plum tomatoes, peeled, seeded, and chopped
1 teaspoon fresh tarragon leaves (or ½ teaspoon dried leaves), chopped
⅓ cup fresh whole wheat breadcrumbs
3 tablespoons feta cheese, chopped (1½ ounces)

IN ADVANCE   Preheat the oven to 350°F.

1.   Place the zucchini in a shallow baking dish and season lightly with salt and pepper. Sprinkle with the lemon juice and chives. Add a tablespoon of water to the dish, cover tightly with foil, and steam the zucchini in the oven while preparing the filling, about 12 to 15 minutes.

2.   Heat the olive oil in a skillet over high heat. Add the scallions and garlic and sauté for about 2 to 3 minutes, stirring frequently.

3. Add the sliced mushrooms to the skillet and continue to sauté, stirring from time to time, for another 4 to 5 minutes. Cook until any liquid released by the mushrooms has evaporated completely.

4. Add the fennel, tomatoes, and tarragon, and sauté for another 3 to 4 minutes, or until the fennel begins to wilt.

5. Remove the skillet from the heat and stir in the breadcrumbs. Fold in the feta cheese, then taste and adjust the seasonings with lemon juice, salt, and pepper to taste.

6. Spoon the filling into the steamed zucchini halves and bake, uncovered, for an additional 15 to 20 minutes. Serve at once.

PREPARATION NOTES

You can prepare the filling up to a day ahead, then cool and refrigerate it overnight. In that case, it is not necessary to prebake the zucchini. Simply spoon the chilled filling into the seasoned zucchini and place in a baking dish. Add a spoonful of water to the dish, cover tightly, then bake, covered, for about 15 minutes. Remove the cover and finish baking for an additional 5 to 6 minutes.

SERVING SUGGESTIONS

Served with a rice or other grain dish, some sautéed greens (kale, spinach, escarole, or collards, for example), or steamed broccoli or shredded cabbage, this dish would make an excellent meatless entrée.

Nutritional information: 130 calories; 5 grams protein; 9 grams fat; 10 grams carbohydrate; 280 milligrams sodium; 10 milligrams cholesterol.

Broiled Belgian Endive with Romesco Sauce

Choose tight heads of Belgian endive that show no scars or blemishes. The tender leaves, which should be a pale ivory color, shaded to a light yellow-green at the tips, should form a tight "point." The Romesco sauce is also excellent with steamed green or white asparagus, cauliflower, or broccoli.

Makes 4 servings

2 dried ancho chilies
1/4 cup extra-virgin olive oil
4 cloves garlic, halved and peeled
1 slice French or Italian bread, cubed
3 plum tomatoes (fresh or canned), peeled, seeded, and chopped
1/2 cup slivered toasted almonds
1/4 cup red wine vinegar
1/2 teaspoon ground cumin
cayenne pepper to taste
salt to taste
black pepper to taste
4 heads Belgian endive
2 teaspoons lemon juice, freshly squeezed

IN ADVANCE Place the chilies in a small bowl and add enough boiling water to cover them completely. Allow them to steep for about 20 minutes, until they are very tender. Remove the stems and seeds and reserve the flesh.

1. Heat 1 tablespoon of the olive oil in a small skillet over low heat. Add the garlic and sauté for about 5 minutes, or until the garlic turns a deep golden brown and releases a rich aroma.

2. Remove the garlic and set aside. In the same oil, sauté the bread cubes until they are evenly toasted.

3. Combine the reserved ancho chilies, the garlic, cubed bread, tomatoes, almonds, vinegar, cumin, and cayenne in a blender. Purée until smooth. Then, with the blender running, add the remaining olive oil. Taste the sauce and add salt and pepper to taste if needed.

4. Trim the bottoms of the endive, leaving them whole, and blanch them by steaming or boiling for a few minutes. Drain the endive well on absorbent toweling. Place in a baking dish, brush each head lightly with a little of the sauce, then broil until very hot about 5 minutes. Serve with additional sauce.

PREPARATION NOTES

Making this sauce can be a little time-consuming, but it can be prepared through step 3, then refrigerated for up to 3 days or frozen for up to 3 months. It can easily be doubled or even tripled so that you can make some for now and freeze some for later.

SERVING SUGGESTIONS

• This dish would make an excellent appetizer. A broiled tuna or swordfish steak would follow such a full-bodied first course well.

• To make this part of a vegetarian meal, serve with a Potato Gratin (see page 226), steamed green beans, and a bean stew (see pages 166 and 168).

Nutritional information: 300 calories; 7 grams protein; 24 grams fat; 20 grams carbohydrate; 145 milligrams sodium; 0 milligrams cholesterol.

Lemon Glaze for Vegetables

In addition to giving vegetables a glossy sheen and a piquant, refreshing flavor, this glaze can be brushed onto chicken or fish as it bakes for a tart, golden glaze, or added to stir-fried vegetables or shellfish for some extra zip.

Makes about 1 cup

2 cups chicken stock
¼ cup lemon juice, freshly squeezed
1 tablespoon grated fresh ginger root
1 teaspoon minced lemon zest
⅛ teaspoon salt
¼ teaspoon cracked black pepper

1. Combine the stock, lemon juice, ginger, and zest. Bring to a boil and reduce to a little less than half the original volume.

2. Add the salt and pepper, cool the glaze, and store in the refrigerator until needed.

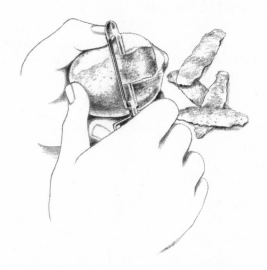

The glaze may be prepared in advance and frozen for up to 3 months. To reheat the glaze, warm it gently over simmering water in the top part of a double boiler, or in a microwave set at half power.

Apply the glaze with a pastry brush to coat items evenly.

To give foods a Caribbean flavor, this glaze can also be prepared with lime juice and zest.

SERVING SUGGESTIONS

Scatter some toasted sesame seeds over glazed foods just before serving.

Nutritional information, per tablespoon: 5 calories; less than 1 gram protein; trace of fat; less than 1 gram carbohydrate; 35 milligrams sodium; trace of cholesterol.

Asparagus with Toasted Anchovy, Garlic, and Lemon

This dish has such a robust flavor that it could easily stand on its own as a first course. For a peasant-style presentation, cut medium-sized spears of asparagus on the bias into 2-inch pieces.

Makes 4 servings

1 pound asparagus
½ teaspoon salt
2 teaspoons extra-virgin olive oil
¼ teaspoon red pepper flakes
2 garlic cloves, sliced thin
6 anchovy fillets, mashed
4 teaspoons lemon juice, freshly squeezed
2 tablespoons chopped fresh flat leaf parsley
freshly ground black pepper to taste

1. Trim the woody ends from the asparagus, and lightly peel about halfway up the stalk. In a skillet, bring about ½ inch of water to a rolling boil. Salt the water and add the asparagus. Cover the pan and steam for about 3 minutes, or until the asparagus is tender, but not soft.

2. Drain the asparagus. (If preparing the asparagus in advance, chill it in ice water, then drain and wrap well. Refrigerate until needed.)

3. Heat the olive oil in a sauté pan over medium heat and add the red pepper flakes and sliced garlic. Sauté until the garlic turns a light golden brown. Add the mashed anchovies and cook until toasted, about 2 minutes.

4. Reheat the asparagus if necessary by steaming or by dropping very briefly into some simmering water. Drain well, then add to the olive oil mixture. Turn the asparagus gently to coat evenly.

5. Add the lemon juice, parsley, and salt to taste. Before serving, grind some black pepper over the asparagus.

To guarantee that the tough asparagus ends are completely removed, hold both ends of the stalk and bend it until it snaps. Note, if you remove asparagus ends by snapping, the remaining stalks will be uneven.

This recipe can also be prepared by substituting the asparagus with broccoli, cauliflower, or green beans for the asparagus.

SERVING SUGGESTIONS

• As part of an antipasto platter you can serve the asparagus either at room temperature or chilled.

• Serve hot on a bed of pasta with some roasted tomatoes, a little extra-virgin olive oil, and plenty of freshly grated Parmesan cheese.

Nutritional information per serving: 80 calories; 4 grams protein; 6 grams fat; 4 grams carbohydrate; 272 milligrams sodium; 10 milligrams cholesterol.

Steamed Spinach with Garlic and Pernod

Raw fresh spinach purchased in "cello packs" has usually been fairly well cleaned, so you'll just need to rinse it well, and remove some of the larger stems. Fresh leaf spinach, on the other hand, requires a great deal of rinsing to remove all traces of sand and dirt. Change the water between rinsings, and continue to rinse until the water is perfectly clean.

Makes 4 servings

1 pound fresh spinach leaves
2 teaspoons unsalted butter
1 garlic clove, minced fine
1 teaspoon shallots, minced
1 teaspoon Pernod
½ teaspoon cracked black peppercorns
¼ teaspoon salt

IN ADVANCE Rinse the spinach leaves well in several changes of water. Drain well or spin dry in a salad spinner.

1. Melt the butter in a skillet over medium heat and add the garlic and shallots. Sauté, stirring frequently, until translucent, about 2 to 3 minutes.

2. Increase the heat to high. Add the spinach leaves a few handfuls at a time, allowing each batch to wilt before adding more.

3. Drizzle the Pernod over the spinach and add the pepper and salt. Toss and serve while still very hot.

The shallots can either be eliminated entirely or replaced with minced yellow onion or the finely sliced white portion of a scallion.

Pernod has a strong licorice flavor, and it may be omitted if its taste is too strong.

SERVING SUGGESTIONS

This would make an excellent bed for a poached fish or sautéed chicken breast. Or serve it as a topping for *foccacio* or other flat breads.

Nutritional information, per serving: 50 calories; 4 grams protein; 3 grams fat; 6 grams carbohydrate; 230 milligrams sodium; 5 milligrams cholesterol.

Pan-steamed Zucchini and Yellow Squash "Noodles"

Cutting vegetables into long thin strips or strands makes it easy to cook them very quickly in just a small amount of water or stock, a technique similar to stir-frying but without any cooking fat.

Makes 4 servings

1 medium zucchini
1 medium yellow squash
1 tablespoon unsalted butter
1 tablespoon minced shallots
1 garlic clove, minced fine
¼ teaspoon cracked black peppercorns
⅓ cup vegetable broth or water
1 tablespoon minced fresh herbs (one or more of the following: basil,
    tarragon, chives, cilantro, thyme, and oregano)
2 teaspoons lemon juice, freshly squeezed

1.   Cut the zucchini and yellow squash into long thin "noodles" by cutting the skin away in long strips, about ¼-inch thick. Cut these strips into long julienne.

2.   Melt the butter in a skillet over medium heat. Add the shallots, garlic, and pepper. Sauté until translucent.

3.   Add squash "noodles" to the pan along with the broth or water. Cover the pan, raise the heat to high, and steam for 2 or 3 minutes, or until the noodles are limp.

4.   Drain away any excess liquid, then add the herbs and lemon juice. (You can also save the liquid to add to stocks, soups, or stews.) Serve at once in a heated serving bowl or on heated plates.

PREPARATION NOTES

Other vegetables that would work in this recipe include carrots, celery, fennel, or leeks (cut into long strands or "noodles"), snow peas (leave whole or cut into slivers), and asparagus (very skinny spears, cut on a long diagonal).

SERVING SUGGESTIONS

• Serve these noodles as a side dish, or as a bed for an entrée that might otherwise benefit from some additional moisture (pan-seared or grilled fish, chicken, or shrimp, for instance).

• To serve this dish as a main course, mound the noodles in the center of a ring of basmati rice. Add large strips of roasted peppers, chopped sun-dried tomatoes, ripe olives, and crumbled fresh goat cheese.

Nutritional information, per serving: 40 calories; 1 gram protein; 3 grams fat; 3 grams carbohydrate; 25 milligrams sodium; 10 milligrams cholesterol.

Vegetable Tempura

Tempura, a cooking technique that calls for foods to be dipped into a batter and then fried until golden, was brought to Japan by Portuguese sailors. The art of tempura was perfected in its adopted home. To ensure that the fried batter will have a crisp, lacy texture, mix the batter right before using it and keep it very cold.

Makes 4 servings

4 cups sliced or diced vegetables: bell peppers, broccoli or cauliflower
    florets, mushrooms, sugar snap or snow peas, zucchini or yellow
    squash, sweet potato, eggplant, onion, scallion
1 egg yolk
1 cup cold water
1 cup all-purpose flour, sifted
¼ cup cornstarch
light sesame, peanut, or corn oil for deep-frying
3 tablespoons dark sesame oil

IN ADVANCE   Add 2 to 3 inches of oil to a wok or deep frying pan. Preheat the oil for deep-frying to 340°F. If you do not have a fryer with a thermostat, or a frying thermometer, check the temperature by dropping a 1-inch cube of bread into the oil. When the temperature is 340°F, the cube will become golden brown in 45 seconds.

1. Steam or blanch the broccoli or cauliflower florets and sweet potato until barely tender. Place them in a bowl of ice water until chilled, drain thoroughly and dry on absorbent toweling.

2. Beat together the egg yolk and ice water. Stir in ¾ cup of the flour and all of the cornstarch to make a smooth batter. Keep cold.

3. Dredge the vegetables in the remaining flour, shaking off any excess.

4. Add the dark sesame oil to the pre-heated deep-frying oil.

5. Turn the vegetable pieces into the batter until evenly coated. Remove them one at a time with a pair of tongs, place the pieces in the hot frying oil, and allow them to deep-fry until golden brown on all sides about 2 to 3 minutes. Remove with a slotted spoon and drain on absorbent toweling.

6. Serve at once with dipping sauce.

PREPARATION NOTES

Make a dipping sauce by blending equal amounts of cold water and soy sauce. Add a teaspoon or two of some or all of the following, to suit your taste: dark sesame oil, mirin (sweetened sake), wasabi powder, grated fresh ginger root, minced garlic, sliced scallions, or *katsuo dashi*. Add grated fresh daikon (a large white radish that can be found with the other Asian vegetables in the produce section of the supermarket), or pass a plate of it so your guests can add their own.

Katsuo dashi is found in Japanese or other Asian markets. It gives a particular smoky, salty taste. It can be omitted if not available in your area.

SERVING SUGGESTIONS

• Served with its traditional dipping sauce, this dish makes an excellent appetizer or first course.

• As the centerpiece of a meal, serve a wide variety of vegetables with plenty of steamed or boiled rice.

• You can also use tempura batter to coat whole shrimp, squid cut into rings, or lean white fish (halibut or scrod) cut into finger-sized pieces.

Nutritional information, per serving (without dipping sauce): 425 calories; 11 grams protein; 19 grams fat; 56 grams carbohydrate; 30 milligrams sodium; 70 milligrams cholesterol.

Green Beans with Sun-dried Tomatoes and Mushrooms

This is another example of a vegetable dish with enough intensity to stand on its own as the start to a meal. It could be served atop slices of a peasant-style bread that has been lightly brushed with olive oil and grilled over a hot fire.

Makes 4 servings

1 pound green beans, trimmed
1½ teaspoons salt
2 tablespoons olive oil
1 garlic clove, minced fine
3 tablespoons slivered sun-dried tomatoes
1 cup sliced wild or domestic mushrooms
¼ teaspoon freshly ground black pepper

1. Put about ½ inch of water in a skillet and bring to a rolling boil over high heat. Add about 1 teaspoon of salt if desired, then add the green beans. Cover the skillet and pan-steam the beans for about 4 minutes, or until they are tender-crisp. Drain the beans and set aside.

2. Lower the heat to medium and add the olive oil to the drained skillet. Add the garlic and sun-dried tomatoes and sauté for about 2 to 3 minutes.

3. Add the mushrooms and raise the heat to high. Sauté, stirring occasionally, until the mushrooms are tender and any juices they release have been cooked away.

4. Return the beans to the pan and toss or stir until they are heated through. Season with salt and pepper and serve at once.

If you can't find sun-dried tomatoes or don't have any on hand when you decide to make this dish, substitute roasted tomatoes, which you can make yourself: Slice ripe tomatoes about ½-inch thick, set on a baking sheet, and roast at 400°F for about 20 minutes or until golden brown.

Replace the garlic with minced shallots, or use roasted garlic if you have some. Instead of olive oil, substitute a minced strip of bacon or pancetta and cook gently over low heat just until some fat is rendered and the bits are crisp.

SERVING SUGGESTIONS

This is a wonderful accompaniment—either as a first course or a side dish—to grilled or baked pork chops, pork roast, roast chicken, or pan-seared salmon or tuna steak.

Nutritional information, per serving: 125 calories; 3 grams protein; 10 grams fat; 10 grams carbohydrate; 360 milligrams sodium; 0 milligrams cholesterol.

Brussels Sprouts with Toasted Walnuts

This tender, nutty-sweet vegetable deserves a second chance. The delicious flavor and unique texture of properly-cooked brussels sprouts is specially enhanced by this recipe. Farmers and gardeners agree that brussels sprouts really come into their own after the first frost. Look in produce markets for the smallest sprouts you can find.

Makes 6 servings

1 pint brussels sprouts
1 teaspoon salt
1 tablespoon walnut oil
¼ cup onions, finely chopped
2 tablespoons red wine vinegar
⅓ cup toasted walnuts, chopped
¼ teaspoon freshly ground black pepper

1. Remove the outer leaves from the brussels sprouts. Score an X in the stem end of each one with a paring knife.

2. Bring about 2 quarts of water to a boil in a saucepan. Salt the water if desired, then add the brussels sprouts. Cook the sprouts for about 8 to 10 minutes, or until they are tender to the bite. Drain the sprouts and set aside.

3. Heat the oil in a skillet over medium heat. Add the onions and sauté, stirring occasionally, until they are limp and have turned a light golden brown.

4. Cut the brussels sprouts into quarters (they may be left whole if they are quite small) and add them to the onions. Toss or stir until they are evenly coated with the walnut oil and heated through.

5. Transfer the brussels sprouts to a heated serving bowl. Sprinkle with the toasted walnuts and serve at once.

Cutting an X in the stem ends of the brussels sprouts allows them to cook more evenly. To test for doneness, pierce the core of the largest sprout with the tip of a paring knife.

The walnut oil gives the brussels sprouts a distinctive nutty aroma and flavor. However, olive, light sesame, or peanut oil could be used instead.

SERVING SUGGESTIONS

This dish would make an excellent accompaniment to roast turkey, capon, pheasant, or cornish game hen, or grilled or sautéed steaks or chops.

Nutritional information, per serving: 90 calories; 4 grams protein; 7 grams fat; 8 grams carbohydrate; 100 milligrams sodium; 0 milligrams cholesterol.

Potatoes

The potato is one of the most resilient and adaptable foods in the world. With just a little care, potatoes can be stored for several weeks, essentially making them a "nonperishable" fresh food. They can be served very simply, and relatively quickly, by boiling, steaming, baking, or cooking in the microwave. These simple preparations deliver a nutritious dish that is naturally low in calories and high in fiber and carbohydrate. The plain "spud" has a sweet, earthy flavor that requires very little adornment.

As a tribute to one of the most beloved and versatile vegetables in this country, we offer here ten recipes for potatoes (including a few for sweet potatoes and yams), ranging from the very simple to the elaborate.

Nutritionally speaking, sweet potatoes and yams provide an additional bonus. Their bright orange or mellow gold flesh contain significant quantities of beta carotene, which our bodies use to produce the Vitamin A that we need. And in spite of their name, sweet potatoes are not significantly higher in calories than white potatoes.

Most shoppers can now find a wider variety of potatoes than they might have in the past. The familiar round red and white potatoes and long, russet baking potatoes are joined by a mellow, butter-colored potato known as a Yukon Gold or Finnish Yellow. These potatoes are not quite as high in starch as russets and Idahos, but they are still delicious when baked. Exotic purple potatoes (the flesh is a dark purple as well) can also be found in some of the larger supermarkets.

The dishes in this chapter offer sound choices for calories-conscious diners. For those recipes that include butter, olive oil, or heavy cream, remember that you can modify the preparation without compromising the flavor of the dish. Either eliminate high-calorie and high-fat ingredients altogether, or make some substitutions: Instead of heavy cream, substitute evaporated skim milk, or a combination of evaporated skim milk and reduced or nonfat sour cream. To reduce calories gained from cooking fat, use a nonstick pan and a very light film of oil instead of sautéing in butter.

Candied Yams with Apples and Bananas

The addition of fruit juices to this dish brightens the flavor and prevents a cloying sweetness. Look for bananas that are a uniform yellow, but that have not begun to brown or soften dramatically. This will help the slices retain their shape during cooking.

Makes 4 servings

3 tablespoons butter
⅓ cup unsweetened apple juice or cider
⅓ cup orange juice
2 tablespoons light brown sugar, lightly packed
small cinnamon stick
1 whole clove
2 allspice berries
¼ teaspoon salt
3 medium yams (about 1 pound), peeled and sliced ½-inch thick
1 Golden Delicious apple, peeled, cored, and sliced ¼-inch thick
1 firm, ripe banana, sliced ½-inch thick
2 tablespoons coarsely chopped roasted peanuts

1. Heat the butter in a large skillet over medium heat. Add the apple and orange juices, sugar, cinnamon stick, clove, allspice berries, and salt, and bring to a boil.

2. Add the yams and reduce the heat until the liquid is barely simmering. Cover the skillet and simmer over very low heat for about 10 minutes.

3. Remove the cover and continue to simmer the yams for another 10 minutes, or until they are barely tender and the liquid is reduced to a golden syrup.

4. Add the apple and banana and heat for another 2 minutes.

5. Serve the yams at once, topped with the chopped peanuts.

PREPARATION NOTES

Although yams and sweet potatoes are not botanically related, they can be used interchangeably in this recipe. Sweet potatoes have a lighter color and more delicate flavor than yams.

SERVING SUGGESTIONS

This potato dish is very rich, and should be paired with an entrée such as marinated grilled meat or chicken, or other simply seasoned foods to provide a contrast.

Nutritional information, per serving: 125 calories; 3 grams protein; 2 grams fat; 26 grams carbohydrate; 100 milligrams sodium; 5 milligrams cholesterol.

Potato Puree with Roasted Eggplant and Garlic

The roasted vegetables give this dish a wonderful texture and flavor. They can be prepared well in advance, making the timing a little less daunting. However, it is best to cook the potatoes exactly when you plan to serve them for the best results.

Makes 6 servings

2 round white potatoes
1 head garlic
1 small eggplant
1/4 cup skim milk
2 tablespoons heavy cream
2 teaspoons olive oil
1/4 teaspoon salt
cayenne pepper to taste

IN ADVANCE Preheat the oven to 375°F.

1. Scrub the potatoes thoroughly and rub them with a little salt. Bake in a 375°F oven for about 1 hour, or until they are very tender.

2. Place the head of garlic on a bed of salt in a small baking dish and roast it along with the potatoes for about 45 minutes. Remove it from the oven when the papery outer skin has turned a deep brown and its juices look brown and have a rich, roasted aroma.

3. Slice the eggplant in half lengthwise and rub the cut side lightly with oil. Place the halves on a baking sheet, cut side down, and roast in a 375°F oven for about 40 minutes (after the potatoes have been in the oven for about 20 minutes). The flesh should be completely cooked and very soft.

4. Using a towel or oven mitt to protect your hands, scoop the flesh from the potatoes and eggplant. Puree it through a sieve or food mill along with two roasted garlic cloves.

5. Bring the skim milk, heavy cream, and olive oil to a boil and add them to the combined purees. Add the salt and cayenne pepper.

6. Serve the puree as soon as possible.

PREPARATION NOTES

For the best results, the potato, eggplant, and garlic should be as warm as possible when they are pureed. The directions for roasting attempts to accommodate the cooking times for each so that everything is done baking at the same time.

It is easiest to roast an entire head of garlic at once. Any unused garlic can be cooled completely, then peeled. Place the cloves in a jar and cover with good-quality olive oil. This will preserve them for later use, and will scent the oil with garlic for use in vinaigrettes or cooking.

SERVING SUGGESTIONS

Use a pastry bag fitted with a star or plain tip to pipe out the puree on each plate in a decorative design.

Nutritional information, per serving: 140 calories; 4 grams protein; 5 grams fat; 21 grams carbohydrate; 120 milligrams sodium; 10 milligrams cholesterol.

Potato Gratin

Casseroled potatoes are notorious for their high calorie and fat contents. With a simple substitution (skim milk for heavy cream) and a moderate hand with cheese, this dish is a good example of how to keep nutrition in mind without sacrificing the quality or texture of your favorite foods.

Makes 6 servings

¾ *cup skim milk*
3 medium baking potatoes, peeled and sliced thin
1 garlic clove, finely minced
¼ *teaspoon salt*
1 teaspoon cornstarch
¼ *cup Gruyère cheese, grated*
3 tablespoons Parmesan cheese, freshly grated
½ *cup fresh white breadcrumbs*

1. Combine the skim milk, potatoes, garlic, and salt in a saucepan. Bring the milk to a simmer over low heat, and continue to cook until the potatoes are nearly tender.

2. Dilute the cornstarch in a small amount of cold water and add it to the simmering milk.

3. Remove the saucepan from the heat and stir in the Gruyère cheese.

4. Transfer the mixture to a 2-inch deep baking dish or casserole and spread in an even layer.

5. Combine the Parmesan cheese and breadcrumbs and sprinkle them evenly over the potatoes.

6. Bake the potatoes in a 350°F oven for about 20 to 30 minutes, or until the top is lightly browned and the potatoes are very tender.

7. Allow the potatoes to rest for about 10 minutes before serving them.

The recipe may be completed through step 4, then refrigerated 2 or 3 hours before baking.

This would serve as an excellent accompainment to the Beef Tenderloin with Blue Cheese and Herb Crust (see page 140), Roast Loin of Pork with a Honey Mustard Glaze (see page 142) or simply with Roasted Chicken.

You could also serve this as part of a brunch menu. Serve with eggs or fresh fruit.

Nutritional information, per serving: 120 calories; 5 grams protein; 3 grams fat; 17 grams carbohydrate; 170 milligrams sodium; 10 milligrams cholesterol.

Celeriac and Potato Puree

Celeriac, also known as celery root, has a knobby, gnarly appearance. Underneath its forbidding exterior lies a faintly sweet, crunchy vegetable that cooks to a soft puree with a mellow celery flavor. This recipe makes the most of its flavor and texture by blending it with potatoes.

Makes 6 servings

2 all-purpose white potatoes, peeled and diced
¾ cup peeled, diced celeriac
¼ cup skim milk
2 tablespoons heavy cream
2 tablespoons unsalted butter
2 teaspoons roasted garlic (optional)
½ teaspoon salt

1. Put the potatoes and celeriac in separate pots, cover with cold water, and bring to a simmer over medium heat. Cook until they are very tender and easy to mash.

2. Drain the potatoes and celeriac. (Optional: To enhance their texture and flavor, place the potatoes and celeriac in an even layer on a baking sheet and steam them dry in a warm oven for about 10 minutes.)

3. Bring the skim milk, heavy cream, and butter to a simmer in a small saucepan on the stovetop, or heat them in the microwave.

4. Puree the potatoes, celeriac, and roasted garlic through a ricer or food mill while hot.

5. Add the puree to the hot milk mixture and fold together (avoid overmixing). Taste and adjust the seasonings with salt.

6. Serve the puree at once in a heated serving bowl or on heated plates.

When you boil potatoes, the way to get the truest flavor is to steam-dry the cooked potatoes. The few minutes spent over low heat or in a warm oven will drive off the extra moisture the potatoes absorbed during cooking. Otherwise, the excess water could dilute the taste, and give a runnier consistency.

To reduce the fat in this recipe, omit the butter and replace the heavy cream with 3 tablespoons of evaporated skim milk.

SERVING SUGGESTION

For a more decorative presentation, fill a pastry bag with the puree and pipe onto plates as a border using a plain or star tip.

Nutritional information, per serving: 100 calories; 2 grams protein; 6 grams fat; 11 grams carbohydrate; 200 milligrams sodium; 17 milligrams cholesterol.

Roësti Potatoes

Traditional roësti calls for generous amounts butter, both clarified and whole. To reduce cholesterol, the clarified butter has been replaced with vegetable oil, and the amount of whole butter has been substantially reduced. Refer to the Preparation Notes following the recipe for further suggestions on how to cut back on fats and calories without losing the wonderful flavor and texture of this crisp potato cake.

Makes 4 servings

3 medium Idaho or russet potatoes
¼ teaspoon salt
¼ teaspoon freshly ground black pepper
2 tablespoons vegetable oil
1 tablespoon unsalted butter

1. Cook the potatoes in their skins in simmering water until they have cooked halfway, about 20 minutes. (The tip of a paring knife inserted into the potato will meet some resistance after the first ½ inch.) Drain the potatoes and allow them to cool until they can be easily handled.

2. Peel the potatoes if desired and grate them with the coarse opening on a box grater. Season them with salt and pepper.

3. Heat the oil in a cast-iron or nonstick skillet over high heat. Add the potatoes and pat them into an even cake. Reduce the heat to medium and cook on the first side for about 5 minutes.

4. Loosen the cake with a metal spatula and dot with butter around the edges. Cook for another 2 to 3 minutes.

5. With the potato cake still in the pan, lay a plate upside down on top of the cake and flip the pan over so that it turns out onto the plate. Then slide the cake back into the pan, uncooked side down.

6. Finish the roësti potatoes over medium heat for another 5 to 6 minutes, or until the second side is golden brown. Slice into wedges and serve at once.

To give this dish a little added interest, blend the grated cooked potatoes with ½ cup grated raw celeriac or carrots, or with finely minced or shredded raw leeks or red onion.

If you prefer, clarified butter can be used to replace some or all of the cooking oil.

To reduce the overall fat content of this dish, use only a teaspoon of oil in a nonstick pan and eliminate the butter. You will need to adjust the temperature carefully to avoid scorching the potatoes.

Once the potatoes have been parcooked, they can be set aside at room temperature for up to an hour or refrigerated for up to 24 hours.

SERVING SUGGESTIONS

• Roësti potatoes are a classic accompaniment to Swiss-style Shredded Veal (see page 124).

• As a lunch or brunch entrée, add slivered smoked ham or salmon to the potatoes and serve with a marinated vegetable salad or Ratatouille (see page 198).

Nutritional information, per serving: 120 calories; 3 grams protein; 7 grams fat; 14 grams carbohydrate; 140 milligrams sodium; trace of cholesterol.

Potatoes Hashed in Cream

A delicious, refined version of hash browns for breakfast or brunch.

Makes 4 servings

3 medium Idaho or russet potatoes
½ cup light cream or half-and-half
¼ teaspoon salt
¼ teaspoon freshly ground black pepper

1. Cook the potatoes in their skins in simmering water until they are cooked halfway, about 20 minutes. (The tip of a paring knife inserted into the potato will meet some resistance after the first ½ inch.) Drain the potatoes and allow them to cool until they can be easily handled.

2. Peel the potatoes and cut them into a medium dice.

3. Bring the cream to a simmer in a skillet and add the diced potatoes. Simmer gently over low heat until the potatoes are cooked through and the cream has thickened to form a sauce, about 10 minutes. Stir gently from time to time to prevent the potatoes and cream from scorching.

4. Season the potatoes with salt and pepper and serve in a heated serving bowl or on heated plates.

PREPARATION NOTES

You can also prepare this recipe using leftover baked or boiled potatoes if you have some on hand.

To reduce the amount of fat in this dish, use evaporated skim milk, or a combination of whole milk and evaporated skim milk.

Use a heat diffuser to help prevent the potatoes and cream from scorching as they cook.

These potatoes could be served with grilled or pan-seared fish, chicken, or pork.

Nutritional information, per serving: 130 calories; 3 grams protein; 4 grams fat; 22 grams carbohydrate; 150 milligrams sodium; 11 milligrams cholesterol.

Glazed Sweet Potatoes

Because of their higher moisture content, sweet potatoes and yams cook more quickly than white potatoes. This recipe offers an interesting sweet-tart contrast, and the pineapple provides a wonderful texture as well.

Makes 6 servings

2 medium sweet potatoes (about 1 pound)
3 to 4 cups water or *broth*
2 cups cubed pineapple (fresh or packed in natural juices)
2 teaspoons lemon juice, freshly squeezed
3 tablespoons honey or *maple syrup*
¼ teaspoon ground cinnamon
2 tablespoons unsalted butter

1. Peel the sweet potatoes and cut them into large dice. Place them in a saucepan with enough water or broth to barely cover and bring to a simmer over medium heat.

2. Reduce the heat to low, cover the pan, and cook the potatoes until they are tender, about 12 to 15 minutes. Drain the potatoes, reserving about 1 cup of the cooking liquid.

3. Add the pineapple, lemon juice, honey, cinnamon, and butter. Continue to cook over low heat stirring gently until the potatoes are coated and glazed. If necessary, add a little of the reserved cooking liquid to prevent the potatoes from becoming too dry.

This recipe can also be prepared with leftover cooked sweet potatoes; simply combine all ingredients in a skillet and heat as described in step 3.

SERVING SUGGESTIONS

Serve these potatoes whenever you would serve white potatoes. They are also a good alternative to rice when serving an entrée of tacos, enchiladas, or burritos.

Nutritional information, per serving: 120 calories; 1 gram protein; 4 grams fat; 21 grams carbohydrate; 6 milligrams sodium; 10 milligrams cholesterol.

Sweet Potato Chips

These bright orange, crunchy chips are addictive. Serve wedges of fresh lemon or lime with the chips, and, for a special taste, drizzle a little freshly squeezed juice on the chips while they are still hot.

Makes 1 pound of chips—8 servings

3 medium sweet potatoes, peeled and sliced thin
peanut or vegetable oil for frying
1 teaspoon salt

IN ADVANCE Preheat 2-3 inches of frying oil to 345°F. A 1-inch cube of bread should fry to golden brown in 65 seconds.

1. Blot the sweet potatoes on absorbent toweling to dry them as much as possible.

2. Heat the frying oil to 325°F and add the sweet potato slices to the pre-heated oil. Stir once or twice with a kitchen fork to keep them from sticking together. Remove the slices using a slotted spoon or spider when they are just barely tender but not brown, about 3 minutes. Blot well on absorbent toweling.

3. Increase the temperature of the oil to 375°F. Return the chips to the oil, stirring once or twice with a kitchen fork to separate the slices. Fry them for about 3 minutes, or until the slices are very crisp and lightly browned.

4. Remove the chips with a slotted spoon or spider and drain on absorbent toweling. Season with salt and serve at once.

PREPARATION NOTES

The best way to get even, thin slices is to use a slicer or a *mandolin*. Otherwise, use the sharpest knife you have and cut them as thinly as possible. Try to keep the slices around ⅛-inch thick.

If you don't have a deep-fryer, use a deep pot or a wok. A deep-fat thermometer is a good idea, since it can otherwise be difficult to gauge the temperature of the oil.

Add the chips to the oil by single handfuls, so that you are only adding enough to cook without crowding. Work in batches if necessary.

SERVING SUGGESTIONS

• These chips make an unusual hors d'oeuvre to accompany cocktails.

• Serve with spicy stews or, for an interesting change, with hamburgers or sandwiches.

Nutritional information, per serving: 130 calories; 2 grams protein; 9 grams fat; 13 grams carbohydrate; 115 milligrams sodium; 0 milligrams cholesterol.

Sweet Potato Cakes

The addition of fresh herbs and capers to these cakes gives them a wonderful piquant flavor. Look for real sweet potatoes, if they are available. They have a lighter yellow flesh and a subtler flavor than bright orange yams.

Makes 4 servings

2 baking potatoes (Idaho or russet), peeled and diced
1 medium sweet potato or yam, peeled and diced
½ cup fresh white breadcrumbs
1 tablespoon mayonnaise
3 tablespoons evaporated skim milk
1 tablespoon capers, rinsed and chopped
1 tablespoon fresh chives, chopped
1 teaspoon fresh dill leaves, chopped
¼ teaspoon salt
¼ teaspoon cracked black pepper

IN ADVANCE   Preheat the oven to 425°F.

1.   Place the potatoes in a pot, add enough water to cover generously, then bring to a simmer over medium heat. Reduce the heat slightly, and continue to simmer until the baking potatoes are very tender, about 15 minutes (cooking time depends on the size of the pieces).

2.   Drain the potatoes in a colander, then return them to the pot. Shake and toss the potatoes for about 3 to 4 minutes over low heat, to eliminate some of the excess moisture.

3.   Put the potatoes through a sieve, ricer, or food mill, or mash them with a potato masher. Add the remaining ingredients and mix well.

4.   Form the mixture into eight cakes of equal size. Place them on a lightly oiled baking sheet and bake in a 425°F oven for 8 to 10 minutes, or until they are lightly browned and very hot. Serve at once.

The sweet potatoes will cook a little more quickly than the white potatoes. To avoid overcooking one or undercooking the other, either cut the white potatoes into a smaller dice than the sweet potatoes, or begin cooking the white potatoes first, and then add the sweet potatoes after about 5 or 6 minutes.

SERVING SUGGESTIONS

This hearty side dish is suitable with braised or stewed meats and baked chicken or fish.

Nutritional information, per serving: 140 calories; 3 grams protein; 2 grams fat; 27 grams carbohydrate; 285 milligrams sodium; trace of cholesterol.

Oven-roasted Potatoes

This tasty version of a traditional potato side dish revises the time-honored technique of cooking potatoes slowly in the fats and juices released by roasting meats. Instead of rolling the potatoes in the rendered meat fats, which tend to be high in saturated fats and cholesterol, a more controlled approach is taken here, using a mono-unsaturated olive oil and plenty of herbs, garlic, and peppercorns to make a highly flavored side dish.

Makes 4 servings

3 baking potatoes (Idaho or russet)
1 tablespoon extra-virgin olive oil
½ teaspoon fresh rosemary leaves, chopped
2 garlic cloves, barely chopped
½ teaspoon cracked black peppercorns
¼ teaspoon salt

IN ADVANCE   Preheat the oven to 375°F.

1.   Scrub the potatoes well and slice them into wedges.

2.   Put the potatoes in a baking dish, and drizzle with the olive oil. Add the remaining ingredients and toss or stir the potatoes until they are evenly coated.

3.   Place the potatoes into the preheated oven and roast for about 35 to 40 minutes, or until the potatoes are tender and golden.

4.   Serve at once in a heated serving dish or on heated plates.

For a spicy variation, substitute sweet potatoes for the baking potatoes and add a little chopped ginger. Replace the rosemary with cilantro or basil. Serve with a wedge of fresh lime.

To prepare on the grill, wrap the seasoned potatoes in a foil packet and place over hot coals. Turn the packet from time to time and cook for about 30 minutes.

SERVING SUGGESTIONS

These potatoes are an excellent accompaniment to roasted or grilled foods. Pass a bottle of malt vinegar to splash on the potatoes while they are still hot.

Nutritional information, per serving: 120 calories; 3 grams protein; 4 grams fat; 140 grams carbohydrate; 285 milligrams sodium; trace of cholesterol.

Desserts

8

In the best of all possible worlds, each meal would be a ritual, a chance to step outside the daily crush of meetings, appointments, deadlines, and demands. We don't always have the luxury of the time involved in planning an entire menu, shopping, and then preparing the meal. If dinner was rushed, and no one had the time to gather together for a three or four-course event, it becomes even more important to sit down together with cup of coffee or tea and a special dessert when the day has at last wound down.

From the kitchens and restaurants of The Culinary Institute of America, we have compiled a sampling of desserts that suit a variety of occasions. The classic tortes, including Sacher Torte, Rum Truffle Torte, and Linzertorte, offer bakers a challenge. The assembly of the various elements of the dessert—including sponge cakes, pastry doughs, syrups, and special fillings and glazes—is a labor of love. It can take several days to prepare all the components, and still another to assemble them. However, this should not deter anyone from preparing a classic dessert, as the individual items are not difficult to make. In addition, most will freeze well or can be refrigerated for at least a few days, or even weeks. This means you can spread the work out to accommodate your schedule. If you are especially organized, you make these building blocks in advance so that they are always on hand, at the ready to produce a dessert virtually on the spot.

If the finished dessert is going to be all that you hoped, it must be built from the choicest ingredients. For example, use the best chocolate and cocoa powder you can find. Nowhere is this more critical than for the

special reduced-calorie and reduced-fat desserts offered in this chapter for which the appealing color and flavor of good-quality chocolate and cocoa—rich, deep, and mellow—enhances the overall effect.

Vanilla extract, heavy cream, butter, and fruits should also be carefully selected. Even an ingredient used in small quantities can have a significant impact on the success of the recipe. Flavorings, nuts, seeds, liqueurs or cordials can make the difference between something that tastes "all right" and something sublime.

For many people, dessert is simply not complete without a steaming cup of coffee, or perhaps a pungent espresso or frothy cappuccino. Still others look for a perfectly brewed pot of tea to draw a meal to a close. These ingredients should also be selected and prepared with the same care used throughout the meal. Look for shops that roast and blend their own coffees and teas. Whenever possible, grind the coffee beans yourself just before brewing them. If you are a tea fancier, try brewing tea loose instead of in bags. Sample a new blend or a special herbal "tisane" from time to time.

Chocolate Yogurt Mousse

Some of the characteristics that make chocolate mousse such a perennial favorite include its smooth texture and melt-away consistency. In this recipe the substitution of drained yogurt for heavy cream and the omission of egg yolks saves about 200 calories and nearly 20 grams of fat without sacrificing either its special chocolate taste or creamy texture.

Makes 6 servings

1 ¼ cups plain nonfat yogurt
1 ½ ounces dark chocolate
4 egg whites
3 tablespoons granulated sugar
¼ cup cocoa powder, sifted twice

IN ADVANCE   To drain the yogurt, line a colander or strainer with a piece of cheesecloth, or a clean linen or cotton cloth or napkin. Place the yogurt in the lined colander, set the colander in a larger bowl or over a plate, and drain for a least 6 hours or overnight in the refrigerator.

Let all of the ingredients come to room temperature before mixing the mousse together.

1. Remove the drained yogurt from the colander and place it in a mixing bowl. Allow it to come to room temperature while melting the chocolate.

2. Heat the chocolate in a microwave at 50-percent power, or over low heat on the stovetop, until melted. Remove it from the heat and allow it to cool to room temperature. Add the chocolate to the yogurt and stir until blended.

3. Combine the egg whites and sugar in a separate bowl, and set the bowl over a pot of simmering water. Heat gently until the sugar crystals have dissolved and the mixture is warm to the touch, or until it reaches a temperature of about 130°F on an instant reading thermometer.

4. Remove the bowl of egg whites from the pot and beat the mixture with an electric mixer until medium peaks form. Fold the beaten egg whites into the chocolate mixture in two parts.

5. Sift the cocoa powder over the mousse, then gently fold it in.

6. Spoon the mousse into serving dishes or molds, and chill for at least 4 hours or overnight before serving.

PREPARATION NOTES

You can drain the yogurt up to 3 days in advance, then store it in a covered container until you are ready to make the mousse.

SERVING SUGGESTIONS

Make a fresh fruit sauce by pureeing ripe strawberries, raspberries, or blackberries until very smooth. For a very fine consistency, put the berries through a fine-mesh sieve to remove any seeds. Then add just enough sugar to very lightly sweeten the sauce, a few drops of fresh lemon juice, and a dash of kirschwasser (a cherry-flavored liqueur) to make an elegant berry coulis. Pool this sauce on a chilled plate and unmold or spoon the mousse onto the sauce.

Nutritional information, per serving: 170 calories; 7 grams protein; 4 grams fat; 31 grams carbohydrate; 80 milligrams sodium; 22 milligrams cholesterol.

Chocolate Angel Food Cake

To make an elegant torte, you could slice this delicate cake into layers, then sandwich them with Chocolate Yogurt Mousse (see page 246). For a professional-looking presentation, drizzle a little melted chocolate in thin criss-cross lines over the top of the cake and chill before serving.

Makes one 10-inch cake

1⅓ cups cake flour
½ cup cocoa powder
1 teaspoon baking powder
12 egg whites
1¾ cups confectioners' sugar, sifted
1 teaspoon cream of tartar
2 tablespoons unsalted butter, melted and cooled
2 teaspoons vanilla extract

IN ADVANCE   Preheat the oven to 325°F.

1.   Combine the flour, cocoa powder, and baking powder, sift twice, and set aside.

2.   Place the egg whites in a mixing bowl and beat with an electric mixer until frothy (use the whip attachment if you have one). With the mixer still running, gradually add the sugar and cream of tartar to the egg whites. Continue to beat the whites until medium peaks begin to form.

3.   Using a spatula, fold the sifted dry ingredients into the beaten egg whites until the batter is evenly blended; then fold in the butter and vanilla extract.

4.   Pour the batter into an ungreased tube pan or springform pan. Bake the cake for about 30 minutes, or until it pulls slightly away from the sides of the pan. Set the cake on a cooling rack, and allow it to cool completely before removing it from the pan.

PREPARATION NOTES

If you are using a tube pan, look to see if it has tiny "feet" on the rim. If it does, you should turn it upside down before cooling the cake. This will help prevent the cake from collapsing as it cools. If your pan doesn't have this feature, invert it over the neck of a wine bottle.

SERVING SUGGESTIONS

• For a simple presentation, dust the cake slices with confectioners' sugar and surround with sliced fresh berries.

• Pool some berry sauce (see the serving suggestions for Chocolate Yogurt Mousse, page 246), and top with a dollop of whipped heavy cream.

Nutritional information, per serving: 90 calories; 3 grams protein; 2 grams fat; 17 grams carbohydrate; 30 milligrams sodium; 5 milligrams cholesterol.

Caramel and Pear Polenta Soufflé

This unusual soufflé recipe replaces the egg yolks, butter, and flour found in the classic formula with a sweetened polenta. The end result has far less fat than a traditional soufflé, but is every bit as flavorful.

Makes 4 servings

½ cup sugar
1 tablespoon cold water
2 ripe pears, cored and peeled
¼ cup pear or apple juice
1 small cinnamon stick
1 whole clove
1¼ cups skim milk
1 strip of orange peel
5 tablespoons cornmeal
3 egg whites

IN ADVANCE Prepare a 1-quart soufflé mold by spraying it lightly with a vegetable oil spray, or by rubbing a little oil over the interior with a paper towel. When you are ready to beat the egg whites, preheat the oven to 400°F.

1. In a small saucepan, dissolve 3 tablespoons of the sugar in the water. Cook the mixture over medium heat until the sugar liquefies and turns a deep caramel brown. Immediately pour the caramel into the prepared mold, leaving a little of the caramel in the pan.

2. Add the pears, juice, cinnamon stick, and clove to the saucepan used to make the caramel. Bring it to a simmer, and poach the pears for about 10 minutes, or until they are very tender.

3. Remove and discard the cinnamon stick and clove. Puree the pears and the cooking juice in blender until very smooth. Set this puree aside.

4. Place the skim milk and orange peel in a separate saucepan. Heat the milk to a simmer and add 3 tablespoons of sugar. Stir until the sugar is completely dissolved. Add the cornmeal in a thin stream, stirring constantly as you pour it.

5.   Add the reserved pear puree to the pan and continue to cook the polenta over low heat for about 20 minutes, stirring frequently, or until it pulls away from the sides of the pot as it is stirred.

6.   Pour the polenta onto a baking dish and cover it with a piece of parchment or waxed paper. Allow the polenta to cool.

7.   Whip the egg whites to a heavy foam, then add the remaining 2 tablespoons of sugar. Continue to beat until the egg whites form medium peaks.

8.   Fold the egg whites into the polenta mixture in two parts, blending just until they are incorporated. Pour the soufflé batter into the caramel-lined soufflé mold.

9.   Place the soufflé mold in a baking dish and place it on the rack in the preheated oven. Add about ¼ inch of hot water to the baking dish, and then bake the soufflé for about 25 minutes, or until it has risen and the top is quite golden.

10.   Remove the soufflé from the oven and serve it immediately from the mold.

PREPARATION NOTES

Making caramel is a tricky operation, and so give it your undivided attention to avoid overcooking the sugar.

The polenta mixture can be prepared through step 6 up to 2 days in advance. Cover it tightly and refrigerate until needed. Allow it to return to room temperature before completing the soufflés.

SERVING SUGGESTIONS

If you prefer to serve four individual soufflés, prepare four 8-ounce molds by spraying them lightly with oil. Distribute the caramel equally among the molds, turning them so that their bottoms are evenly coated. The baking time will be reduced to about 15 to 16 minutes.

Nutritional information, per serving: 185 calories; 5 grams protein; 1 gram fat; 40 grams carbohydrate; 65 milligrams sodium; trace of cholesterol.

Winter Fruit Strudel

Strudels are easy to prepare from frozen packaged, phyllo dough. These thin pastry sheets can be found in the frozen-foods section of many grocery stores. If you keep a few boxes in your freezer, making sweet strudels like this one can become simple and convenient. They are always well-received.

Makes 8 servings

¼ cup chopped pitted prunes
¼ cup chopped dried apricots
¼ cup raisins
2 tablespoons brandy or dark rum
¼ cup boiling water
4 Granny Smith apples, cored, peeled, and diced
2 pears, cored, peeled, and diced
5 teaspoons brown sugar, lightly packed
2 tablespoons pecans or walnuts, toasted and chopped
¼ teaspoon ground nutmeg
¾ teaspoon ground cinnamon
8 sheets phyllo dough
4 teaspoons butter, melted (or a nut oil—hazelnut, walnut, or almond)

1. Combine the prunes, apricots, and raisins in a small bowl. Add the brandy and boiling water to the fruit and allow it to plump for about 30 minutes.

2. Combine the apples, pears, sugar, nuts, nutmeg, and cinnamon in a large bowl, and toss to coat the fruit with the sugar and spices.

3. Add the dried fruit and its plumping liquid to the apple and pear mixture and toss until blended. Spread this mixture in an even layer in a baking pan and cover loosely with parchment paper or aluminum foil.

4. Bake the fruit for about 35 to 40 minutes in a 350° oven, or until they are very tender. Remove from the oven and allow to cool.

5. Stack two sheets of phyllo on a flat work surface and brush lightly with a little of the melted butter. Top with another two sheets, and brush with butter, and repeat until all the phyllo sheets are stacked up and brushed with butter.

6. Mound the baked fruit along one of the long edges of the dough, then roll the strudel. Brush the rolled strudel with a little butter, then use a sharp knife to very lightly score its top.

7. Set the strudel on a baking sheet and bake in a 425°F oven for about 25 minutes, or until the dough is a golden brown.

8. Let the strudel cool slightly before slicing and serving.

PREPARATION NOTES

The strudel can be prepared through step 6, and then wrapped and frozen. To bake it directly from the freezer, bake the strudel at 375°F for 30 minutes, then increase the heat to 425°F for the final 10 minutes of baking.

You can substitute your favorite dried fruits for the prunes and apricots suggested here. Try adding a few dried cranberries or blueberries, or add chopped dried apple rings to enhance the apple flavor in the strudel.

SERVING SUGGESTIONS

Whipped cream or vanilla ice cream are perfect accompaniments to this dish. To avoid their calories and extra fat, serve with nonfat frozen yogurt.

Nutritional information, per serving: 100 calories; 1 gram protein; 1 gram fat; 24 grams carbohydrate; trace of sodium; trace of cholesterol.

Tarte Tatin, St. Andrew's Style

In this recipe, the buttery pastry layer of the classic tarte tatin has been replaced with a tender ricotta cheese dough, which provides the rich flakey consistency of the classic version without a lot of butter. Paired with caramelized fruit, this is a fine example of a delicious—and nutritionally conscious—dessert.

Makes 8 to 10 servings

6 tablespoons granulated sugar
1 tablespoon unsalted butter
6 Granny Smith apples, peeled, cored, and sliced
1 recipe Sweet Ricotta Pastry (see page 256)

IN ADVANCE   Preheat the oven to 350°F.

1.   Place the sugar in a large skillet and cook it over medium heat until it liquifies and turns into a light caramel.

2.   Add the butter and apple slices and toss the apples in the caramel over medium heat until they are well-coated.

3.   Remove the pan from the heat and arrange the apple slices in neat concentric rings in the pan.

4.   Roll out the pastry dough into a ½-inch-thick circle large enough to cover the entire pan. Cut vents in the pastry, then place it in the pan on top of the apples. Press the pastry dough down onto the apples.

5.   Bake the tarte in a 350°F oven for about 30 minutes, or until the crust is golden brown.

6.   Loosen the crust from the sides of the pan. Place a platter over the top of the tarte, then flip the pan to transfer the tarte to the plate.

7.   Allow the tarte to cool slightly, then cut into wedges and serve.

If you wish to prepare the tarte in advance, cook the apples as directed in steps 1 and 2, then transfer the apples to a freezer-safe casserole dish. Roll out the dough and top the apples as directed in step 4, then wrap the tarte tightly and freeze. To bake without thawing, increase the baking time to about 50 minutes and keep the tarte covered with foil during the first 20 minutes.

You may replace some or all of the apples with pears.

SERVING SUGGESTIONS

While frozen nonfat yogurt would be a logical choice to accompany this trimmed-down version of a classic dessert, you could certainly indulge yourself with a little whipped cream without "wrecking" its nutritional pluses.

Nutritional information, per serving: 155 calories; 2 grams protein; 3 grams fat; 33 grams carbohydrate; 100 milligrams sodium; 10 milligrams cholesterol.

Sweet Ricotta Pastry

This dough can be prepared by hand (see the Preparation Notes below), or it can be prepared in a food processor. Try to keep the ingredients and the dough as cool as possible during mixing and shaping. The temperature of the dough will determine the tenderness of the baked dessert.

Makes about ¾ pound of dough (enough for 1 Tarte Tatin)

2 cups all-purpose flour, sifted
¼ cup granulated sugar
1 tablespoon baking powder
⅛ teaspoon salt
½ cup part-skim ricotta, well-chilled
3 tablespoons skim milk, chilled
1 egg white, chilled
2 tablespoons unsalted butter, diced and chilled
½ teaspoon vanilla extract

1. Combine the flour, sugar, baking powder, and salt in the bowl of a food processor fitted with a steel blade. Process these ingredients for about 15 seconds, or until they are blended.

2. Add the ricotta, skim milk, egg white, butter, and vanilla extract through the feed tube, and pulse the machine on and off, mixing just long enough for the dough to develop into a shaggy mass.

3. Turn the dough out onto a lightly flour work surface and gently pat it into a ball. Wrap the dough and chill it in the for at least 1 hour.

4. Roll the dough out as directed to prepare Tarte Tatin (see page 254), or for another baked dessert.

To mix the dough by hand, combine all of the dry ingredients in a large bowl, and stir to distribute the baking soda and salt evenly. Cut the butter into the flour. Blend the cheese, milk, egg white, and vanilla. Add them to the dough and stir just until the dough adheres into a shaggy mass. Knead dough gently 2 or 3 times to form a ball. Do not overknead the dough; it should remain cool to the touch. Continue with step 3 above.

SERVING SUGGESTIONS

In addition to its use in the recipe for Tarte Tatin, this dough can be used to prepare other desserts, including fruit turnovers and deep-dish pies.

Nutritional information, per serving: 65 calories; 2 grams protein; 1 gram fat; 10 grams carbohydrate; 85 milligrams sodium; 5 milligrams cholesterol.

Linzertorte

Cake crumbs are a constant commodity in a professional bakeshop, and recipes such as this one offer a way to use up what would otherwise be thrown away. If you don't have cake crumbs on hand, and don't want to bake a cake just to make them, substitute an equal measure of breadcrumbs made from crustless white bread and increase the sugar by about 1 tablespoon.

Makes one 9-inch round torte

¾ cup unsalted butter, at room temperature
½ cup granulated sugar
1 whole egg
½ teaspoon vanilla extract
¾ cup ground toasted hazelnuts, walnuts, or almonds
½ cup fine cake crumbs
2 cups cake flour
½ teaspoon cinnamon powder
½ teaspoon baking powder
½ cup raspberry jam
1 egg yolk
1 tablespoon milk

IN ADVANCE Lightly butter or spray with vegetable oil a 9-inch round tart pan with a removable bottom. Preheat the oven to 375°F.

1. Combine the cake flour, cinnamon powder, and baking powder and sift together twice. Set aside until needed.

2. Combine the butter and sugar in a bowl, and cream well by hand or with an electric mixer until the mixture is very smooth and light. Scrape the bowl down to be sure that the butter and sugar are properly mixed.

3. Add the egg and vanilla and continue to beat until the batter is quite light and smooth.

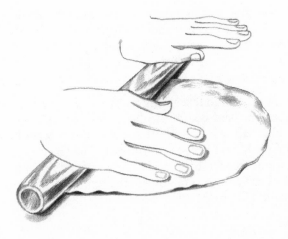

4. Add the ground nuts, cake crumbs, and the sifted dry ingredients from step 1. Blend by hand or with the paddle attachment of an electric mixer until they well combined.

5. Gather the dough into a ball, wrap well, and refrigerate for 1 hour before rolling it out.

6. Cut away about one-third of the dough and return it to the refrigerator. Roll out the remaining dough on a lightly floured work surface to form a 10-inch-wide circle. Fit the dough into the prepared tart pan, pressing it into the corners and sides of the pan.

7. Spread the raspberry jam over the surface of the dough.

8. Roll out the remaining dough into a 9-inch-long, ¼-inch-thick rectangle. Cut into strips and arrange them on the surface of the tart to make a lattice top. Crimp the edges of each strip to seal them to the bottom crust.

9. Blend the egg yolk and milk in a dish, then brush the egg wash on the lattice. Preheat the oven to 375°F.

10. Bake the tart for about 30 to 35 minutes. Allow it to cool completely on a rack before removing it from the pan. Slice the torte, dust with confectioners' sugar, and serve.

PREPARATION NOTES

The recipe for the dough (excluding the jam and egg wash) can easily be doubled. The unbaked dough can be frozen for later use.

Another alternative is to completely assemble the tart (do not brush it with the egg wash) and freeze it in the pan. The tart can then be baked directly from the freezer; bake at 350°F for about 45 minutes. If the tart appears to be browning too rapidly on the top, cover it loosely with foil and reduce the heat to 325°F.

SERVING SUGGESTIONS

Ideally, this tart should be allowed to rest for two days to reach the peak of its flavor and moist texture, with an intense aroma of raspberries and nuts. Wrap the cooled tart tightly and store it in a cool, dry place until ready to serve.

Nutritional information, per serving: 375 calories; 5 grams protein; 22 grams fat; 41 grams carbohydrate; 25 milligrams sodium; 90 milligrams cholesterol.

Coffee Granité

Granité is meant to have a coarse, icy texture. It is simple to prepare and does not require an ice cream freezer.

Makes about 6 servings

3½ cups water
2¼ cups granulated sugar
1 cup strong brewed espresso
1 egg white, beaten to a light froth

1. Combine the water and sugar in a saucepan over high heat. Bring the mixture to a boil, stirring frequently, until the sugar has dissolved. Reduce the heat slightly and continue to simmer for 5 minutes.

2. Remove the sugar mixture from the heat. Add the espresso and let cool to room temperature.

3. Stir the egg white into the coffee mixture just until blended. Do not whip. Pour the mixture into a shallow pan and place it in the freezer.

4. When the granité is frozen, use a metal spoon to scrape the surface, creating its coarse, trademark crystals. Serve in chilled bowls, cups, or glasses.

PREPARATION NOTES

If you prefer a smoother texture, freeze the cooled granité mixture in an ice cream machine. Process according to the manufacturer's directions.

SERVING SUGGESTIONS

Granité can be served as an accompaniment to a variety of small cookies, or with a selection of fresh fruits.

Nutritional information, per serving: 290 calories; 1 gram protein; trace of fat; 75 grams carbohydrate; 15 milligrams sodium; 0 milligrams cholesterol.

Frozen Orange Soufflé

Frozen soufflés offer a dessert option that can be prepared well in advance of your dinner party, eliminating the need for any last-minute fussing. You can serve this soufflé from a number of containers—a soufflé dish (either individual molds or a single, larger one), hollowed-out oranges, or stemmed wine glasses.

Makes 6 soufflés

2 whole eggs
2 egg yolks
1 cup granulated sugar
3 tablespoons Grand Marnier
1¼ cups heavy cream, chilled

IN ADVANCE   To make a paper collar for the soufflé mold, cut a strip of waxed or parchment paper wide enough to wrap around the mold, leaving enough for a 2-inch overlap. Tape it securely in place.

Whip the heavy cream until medium peaks form and keep in the refrigerator until needed.

1.   Place the whole eggs and yolks in a mixing bowl. Add the sugar and beat lightly to blend. Set the bowl over a pot of simmering water and continue to stir frequently until the egg mixture is heated, or until it reaches a temperature of about 130°F on an instant reading thermometer.

2.   Remove the egg mixture from the heat and beat it with an electric mixer until it has nearly tripled in volume and forms ribbons that sit on the surface of the batter without "melting" immediately.

3.   Add the Grand Marnier along with half of the whipped cream. Fold the cream gently into the batter until evenly blended. Add the remaining cream and fold it into the batter.

4. Pour the batter into the prepared mold, and then freeze for several hours or overnight.

5. Remove the soufflé from the freezer, remove the collar, and serve.

PREPARATION NOTES

You can use other cordials to prepare this soufflé: Kahlua or Tia Maria for a coffee flavor, Frangelico for hazelnut, and Amaretto for almond. You can also add a small amount of a fruit puree (raspberry, strawberry, or banana) in place of the Grand Marnier in step 3.

SERVING SUGGESTIONS

Serve the soufflé with a dollop of whipped heavy cream, or accompany with well-chilled sliced oranges or other fresh seasonal fruits.

Nutritional information, per serving: 365 calories; 4 grams protein; 22 grams fat; 37 grams carbohydrate; 45 milligrams sodium; 250 milligrams cholesterol.

Rum Truffle Torte

This torte is assembled from several different components, all of which can be prepared in advance. Having plain sponge cakes, and a few prepared doughs ready and stored in the freezer makes it simple to prepare elegant desserts. You may want to brush the layers of frozen sponge cake with Simple Syrup to help restore any moisture that was lost during freezing.

Makes 10 to 12 servings

one 10-inch layer of Linzertorte dough, (see page 258)
one 10-inch Chocolate Sponge Cake (see page 272)
6 ounces chocolate, semi-sweet or dark
¾ cup heavy cream
2 tablespoons unsalted butter
2 cups cake crumbs
1 tablespoon marzipan or almond paste
¾ cup seedless raspberry jam
2 tablespoons apricot jam
¼ cup dark rum

IN ADVANCE Roll the Linzertorte dough into an even circle 10 inches in diameter. Bake it on a lightly oiled baking sheet for 10 to 12 minutes at 350°F or until light brown at the edges. Slice the sponge cake horizontally into three thin layers.

1. Combine the chocolate, heavy cream, and butter in a small saucepan and bring the mixture to a simmer over medium heat. Remove the pan from the heat and stir until the chocolate is evenly distributed. Allow this glaze to cool to room temperature.

2. To make the filling, place the crumbs, marzipan, ⅓ cup raspberry jam, apricot jam, and rum in the bowl of a food processor fitted with a steel blade. Process until the mixture is crumbly.

3. With the processor running, add ¾ cup of the chocolate mixture to the filling through the feed tube, and continue to process until evenly blended.

4. To assemble the torte, spread the linzer dough with half of the filling. Place a layer of the sponge cake on top of the filling, then spread the remaining raspberry jam on top. Place a second layer of sponge cake on top of the jam and coat it with the remaining filling. Top with the remaining layer of sponge cake.

5. If the chocolate glaze has hardened, heat it over low heat until it is warm enough to pour easily. Set the assembled torte on a cooling rack set over a baking sheet. Brush away any crumbs from the sides and top of the cake.

6. Spread a very thin layer of the glaze over the sides and top of the cake and let the excess drip off. Put the cake in the freezer for 15 minutes to firm up the glaze. Reheat the remaining glaze if necessary, and then pour it over the torte, spreading the glaze quickly with a spatula to completely coat the cake.

PREPARATION NOTES

The filling can be prepared in advance and refrigerated for 3 or 4 days or frozen for up to 2 months. The sponge cake and the linzer torte dough can be baked and then frozen for several weeks as well. The chocolate glaze can also be prepared in advance and refrigerated for up to 10 days.

SERVING SUGGESTIONS

Decorate the top of the cake with rum-flavored truffles. (Refer to the recipe for Chocolate Glaze (page 276) for preparation instructions.)

Nutritional information, per serving: 490 calories; 8 grams protein; 17 grams fat; 78 grams carbohydrate; 310 milligrams sodium; 200 milligrams cholesterol.

Sacher Torte

This dessert is one of Vienna's most famous. There was actually a court case, settled only after many years of wrangling, to decide which of two of the city's renowned hotels could claim ownership of the original recipe.

Makes one 10-inch cake

1 cup plus 6 tablespoons unsalted butter, at room temperature
1⅓ cups confectioners' sugar
2 whole eggs
8 egg yolks
8 ounces unsweetened chocolate, melted and cooled
8 egg whites
½ cup bread flour
1¾ cups ground toasted almonds
½ cup strained apricot or raspberry jam
¼ cup heavy cream
Chocolate Glaze or Sauce (see page 276)

IN ADVANCE   Rinse a bowl with white vinegar and then with hot water to remove all traces of grease before whipping the egg whites in step 4. Lightly oil a 10-inch springform pan. Preheat the oven to 350°F.

1.   Cream the butter together with 1 cup of the sugar by hand or with an electric mixer until very smooth and light.

2.   Add the whole eggs and yolks to the creamed butter mixture and beat well until smooth and light. Scrape the bowl down to make sure that the mixture is evenly blended.

3.   Add the chocolate and mix well.

4. In a separate bowl, beat the egg whites until thick and foamy. Add the remaining confectioners' sugar one tablespoon at a time and continue to whip until the egg whites form medium peaks.

5. Add the beaten egg whites to the chocolate mixture in two parts, folding gently with a spatula.

6. Add the flour and almonds to the batter, folding them into the chocolate mixture just until blended.

7. Pour the batter into a prepared baking pan and bake in a preheated oven for 25 minutes, or until it springs back when lightly pressed with a fingertip and the edges have pulled away from the pan.

8. Cool the cake in the pan on a rack for at least 15 minutes, then unmold it to complete cooling.

9. Slice the cake horizontally. Spread a layer with the preserves, then top with the other layer. Brush away any loose crumbs from the sides and top of the cake.

10. Set the cake on a rack and pour warm chocolate glaze over the top. Use a spatula to smooth out the top and to coat the sides. Allow the glaze to firm for several hours at room temperature before slicing and serving.

PREPARATION NOTES

The cake should not be refrigerated, in order to maintain the glaze's sheen. The uncut cake will stay fresh for up to 3 days.

SERVING SUGGESTIONS

A pool of berry puree (see the notes following the recipe for Chocolate Yogurt Mousse, page 246), a dollop of whipped cream, or some fresh berries would all be appropriate with this dessert. Once cut, the cake may be refrigerated.

Nutritional information, per serving: 540 calories; 10 grams protein; 40 grams fat; 38 grams carbohydrate; 60 milligrams sodium; 290 milligrams cholesterol.

Petits Pots de Crème

With a texture somewhere between a mousse and a custard, *pots de crème* are traditionally served in ceramic custard cups with lids. If you can find chocolate-coated coffee beans, use them to garnish each serving, along with a dollop of freshly whipped cream.

Makes 8 servings

1½ cups sugar
1½ cups milk
1½ cups heavy cream
3 egg yolks
3 whole eggs
3 ounces semi-sweet or dark chocolate, melted
1½ teaspoons vanilla extract

IN ADVANCE Combine the milk and cream in a small pan and warm it gently over low heat while cooking the caramel in step 1. Preheat the oven to 325°F.

1. Place 1 cup of the sugar in a medium saucepan and cook over medium heat without stirring until it liquefies and turns a deep caramel color. If there are sugar crystals on the sides of the pan above the level of the melted sugar, dip a pastry brush in water and wash down the sides of the pan.

2. Add the warmed milk and cream to the caramel and bring the mixture to a boil. Stir well to completely dissolve the caramel.

3. Beat together the remaining ½ cup of sugar with the whole eggs and yolks in a small bowl. Add about ½ cup of the hot milk mixture and blend well. Add another ½ cup and stir, then pour the entire mixture back into the saucepan.

4. Continue to heat the milk and egg mixture for another 2 minutes over low heat. Do not allow the mixture to boil. Strain it through a fine sieve into a bowl.

5. Add the chocolate and vanilla extract and stir until the chocolate is completely melted. Ladle the mixture into custard cups and cover with lids, aluminum foil, or waxed paper.

6. Place the filled custard cups in a baking dish and add enough boiling water to come up to the level of the pots de crème. Place the pan in the preheated oven and cook until the mixture is just set (the tip of a knife inserted near the center of the custard cup should come out clean), for about 20 minutes.

7. Remove the custard cups from the water bath. Allow the petits pots de crème to cool, then refrigerate until firm, or overnight.

PREPARATION NOTES

Use some care when adding the warmed milk and cream to the hot caramel. It is quite likely that there will be some splattering when the liquid hits the very hot sugar.

SERVING SUGGESTIONS

This dessert needs nothing more than a small rosette of whipped cream.

Nutritional information, per serving: 435 calories; 7 grams protein; 26 grams fat; 47 grams carbohydrate; 70 milligrams sodium; 270 milligrams cholesterol.

Crème Brulée

Although its French name is rather misleading, this dessert was originally developed at Cambridge in England, where it was known as
"burnt cream." Many contemporary chefs use blow torches instead of
the traditional salamander to caramelize the sugar topping.

Makes 6 servings

2½ cups heavy cream
1 vanilla bean
1 cup granulated sugar (plus more as needed for a topping)
5 egg yolks
1 whole egg

IN ADVANCE   Lightly butter six 4-ounce custard cups. Preheat the
oven to 325°F.

1.   Combine the heavy cream, vanilla bean, and ½ cup sugar in a
saucepan. Bring the mixture to a boil over high heat, then reduce the
heat to low.

2.   Beat the egg yolks, whole egg, and the remaining ½ cup of sugar
together in a small bowl. Add about ½ cup of the hot heavy cream and
stir well. Return the entire mixture to the saucepan and continue to
cook over low heat for another 2 minutes. Strain this custard mixture
through a sieve into the prepared custard cups, filling them to within ¼
inch of the top.

3. Place the filled custard cups in a baking dish and add enough boiling water to come up to the level of the custard in the cups. Place the baking dish in the preheated oven, then cook the custard in the water bath for about 30 minutes, or until just barely set (the tip of a knife should come out clean when inserted near the center of the custard).

4. Remove the custard cups from the water bath, cool them to room temperature, then refrigerate them until firm or overnight.

5. Completely cover the surface of each custard with an even ⅛-inch-thick layer of sugar. Preheat the broiler. Place the custards in a baking dish filled with crushed ice or ice water.

6. Cook the custard under the broiler until the sugar liquefies and turns a dark caramel. Serve at once.

PREPARATION NOTES

The ice bath used in step 6 prevents the custard from heating up as the sugar topping is caramelized.

SERVING SUGGESTIONS

This dessert is a fitting conclusion to a meal that features highly spiced, grilled, or roasted foods.

Nutritional information, per serving: 600 calories; 5 grams protein; 42 grams fat; 52 grams carbohydrate; 60 milligrams sodium; 410 milligrams cholesterol.

Chocolate Sponge Cake

This basic recipe can be easily varied to create cakes with special flavors (see Preparation Notes). If you have a large mixer, make a double batch of the batter, bake the layers, then freeze some for later. Brush the layers with Simple Syrup before filling and frosting for a dense, moist cake or torte.

Makes one 10-inch cake

1 cup sifted cake flour
⅓ cup cocoa powder
¼ cup cornstarch
6 whole eggs
1½ cups granulated sugar
¼ cup unsalted butter, melted and cooled
½ teaspoon vanilla extract

IN ADVANCE Preheat the oven to 350°F. Coat a 10-inch spring-form cake pan with oil or butter, then coat with flour and remove any excess.

1. Combine the flour, cocoa powder, and cornstarch and sift twice. Set these dry ingredients aside.

2. Combine the eggs and sugar in a mixing bowl and set the bowl over a pot of simmering water. Heat the egg mixture, stirring frequently, until is warm to the touch, or reaches a temperature of 130°F on an instant reading thermometer.

3. Remove the egg mixture from the pot and whip with an electric mixture until the eggs have tripled in volume (use the whip attachment if you have one). The batter should fall in ribbons that sit on the surface of the batter without melting away immediately.

4. Sift the dry ingredients over the surface of the batter and fold them in with a spatula. Drizzle the butter and vanilla extract over the batter and gently fold them in as well.

5. Pour the batter into the prepared cake pans and bake for about 20 to 25 minutes, or until the cake has begun to shrink away from the pan slightly.

6. Remove the cake from the oven and let it cool in its pan for 15 minutes. Then, loosen the cake from the sides of the pan, unmold, and cool it completely on a cake rack.

7. At this point the cake is ready to be filled and frosted.

PREPARATION NOTES

This cake freezes well, and can be stored, well-wrapped, for up to 2 months.

To vary the flavor of this cake, make the following changes or substitutions: For mocha, add 2 tablespoons of instant espresso, diluted in 1 tablespoon of boiling water. For a plain cake, omit the cocoa powder and replace it with ⅓ cup cake flour. Plain cakes can be flavored with 2 teaspoons lemon or orange extract, 1 teaspoon almond extract. Add up to ½ cup ground toasted nuts to either plain or flavored cakes for additional texture and flavor.

SERVING SUGGESTIONS

In addition to simply topping it with whipped cream and sliced berries for a quick dessert, this sponge cake can be used to prepare a number of other desserts (see the recipe for Rum Truffle Torte, page 000).

Nutritional information, per serving: 260 calories; 5 grams protein; 9 grams fat; 42 grams carbohydrate; 45 milligrams sodium; 175 milligrams cholesterol.

Strawberry Pecan Shortcake

Although the recipe instructions for mixing this shortcake call for a food processor, it is just as easy to mix the dough by hand. Simply use a pastry blender or two table knives to combine the butter with the dry ingredients, and mix the cream in with a fork.

Makes 4 servings

2 pints fresh strawberries, sliced
¾ cup sugar
1½ cups all-purpose flour, sifted
½ cup finely ground pecans, toasted
¾ teaspoon salt
¾ teaspoon baking powder
3 tablespoons unsalted butter, diced and chilled
¾ cup heavy cream, chilled

IN ADVANCE   Preheat the oven to 350°F.

1.   Place the berries in a bowl. Sprinkle with 4 tablespoons of the sugar and toss to coat evenly. Allow the berries to sit for at least 1 hour.

2.   To make the biscuits, place the flour, pecans, salt, baking powder, and the remaining sugar in the bowl of a food processor fitted with a steel blade. Run the machine for about 30 seconds to blend the ingredients evenly.

3.   Add the butter and pulse the machine on and off until the mixture looks like a coarse meal.

4. With the machine running, quickly add the heavy cream and continue to process just until a shaggy mass is formed.

5. Turn the dough out onto a floured work surface, divide it evenly into four pieces, then pat them into round biscuits. Place the cakes on a lightly oiled baking sheet and bake for about 30 to 35 minutes, or until golden brown.

6. Split the biscuits in half and spoon the strawberries over the bottom half of each one, cover with the top half, then place a dollop of cream on each serving.

PREPARATION NOTES

Add other berries to the sweetened strawberries as they come into season, or try sliced ripe peaches or apricots later in the summer.

To reduce the overall calories and fat, substitute a slice of plain angel food cake for the biscuit and use just a little dollop of whipped heavy cream.

SERVING SUGGESTIONS

Use a pastry bag fitted with a star tip to pipe out the whipped cream for a more elegant presentation.

Nutritional information, per serving: 570 calories; 7 grams protein; 34 grams fat; 63 grams carbohydrate; 800 milligrams sodium; 70 milligrams cholesterol.

Chocolate Glaze or Sauce

A good-quality chocolate will give this glaze a sheen and excellent taste. The best chocolates will appear glossy, and will melt readily when you taste them. The baking section of larger supermarkets, candy-making supply shops, and gourmet food stores will offer a selection of dark, bittersweet, milk, and white chocolates for baking and eating.

Makes 2 cups of glaze

1 cup heavy cream
¼ cup sugar
2 tablespoons butter
6 ounces dark chocolate, chopped
Flavored liqueur (optional; dark rum, Kahlua, Grand Marnier,
   Frangelico, Amaretto), to taste

1. Combine the heavy cream and sugar in a saucepan and bring to a boil over medium heat. Immediately remove the pan from the heat.

2. Add the butter and chocolate to the hot cream and stir constantly until the chocolate has melted.

3. Add the liqueur to taste. Serve the glaze or sauce as desired.

To use it as a glaze, place the item to be coated on a rack, brush any loose crumbs from the surface, and coat with the glaze.

This recipe can be easily be doubled or tripled and refrigerated in a covered jar for up to 10 days. Warm it gently over low heat, either in the top of a double boiler or in the microwave, before using.

SERVING SUGGESTIONS

• Serve as a sauce pooled beneath a dessert or as a topping for ice cream.

• To make truffles, chill the sauce, break off small pieces, then quickly roll them into uneven balls. Roll the balls in cocoa powder. These truffles can be served as is, or used to decorate the Rum Truffle Torte (see page 264).

Nutritional information, per serving: 130 calories; 1 gram protein; 11 grams fat; 9 grams carbohydrate; 10 milligrams sodium; 25 milligrams cholesterol.

Simple Syrup

Since a sponge cake does not have the large quantities of butter that are found in many traditional layer cakes, this syrup can provide the necessary moistness.

Makes 2 cups

2 cups water
1 cup sugar
2 thick slices of orange
1 slice of lemon

1. Combine all of the ingredients in a saucepan and bring to a boil over high heat, stirring frequently.

2. Dip a pastry brush in cold water and wash down the sides of the pan to dissolve any sugar crystals.

3. Reduce the heat to low and simmer for another 5 minutes. Remove and discard the orange and lemon slices. Let the syrup cool slightly, then pour into a clean jar. Use as needed.

PREPARATION NOTES

The syrup can be refrigerated for up to 3 months. It can be used to poach fruits, or to sweeten drinks such as iced tea especially if the liquid is already cold and granulated sugar might not dissolve easily.

To apply simple syrup to a sponge cake, dip a pastry brush into the syrup (cold or room temperature) and daub it over the surface of the cake to evenly moisten each layer.

SERVING SUGGESTIONS

For a special flavor, add a small amount of liqueur, dark rum, or vanilla extract to the syrup before brushing it onto the cake.

Nutritional information, per tablespoon: 50 calories; 0 grams protein; 0 grams fat; 13 grams carbohydrate; trace of sodium; 0 milligrams cholesterol.

Index